Eurocommunism
and
Foreign Policy

Carole Webb

Studies in European Politics 4

Acknowledgements

The author would like to acknowledge her debt to the following: to Lily Marcou at the Centre d'Études et des Recherches Internationales, Fondation Nationale des Sciences Politiques, Paris, for the benefit of her knowledge of the international communist movement; to Chatham House Press Library; to the Department of European Studies at UMIST for support—in particular, Mrs Liz Diggle for typing the manuscript; and, lastly, to colleagues, friends and husband Martin Webb for their patient help and interest. Errors and omissions remain the sole responsibility of the author.

ISBN 0-85374-174-3

Published by Policy Studies Institute, 1-2 Castle Lane, London SW1E 6DR
Printed by Dawson & Goodall Ltd., Bath, England

Contents

Studies in European Politics

This series provides brief and up-to-date analyses of European political issues, including developments in the European Community and in transnational political forces, and also major problems in particular European countries. The research is undertaken by the European Centre for Political Studies, established in 1978 at the Policy Studies Institute with the sponsorship of the European Cultural Foundation. The series is edited by the Head of the Centre, Dr Roger Morgan.

Studies published in 1979

1. The Future of the European Parliament   *David Coombes*

2. Towards Transnational Parties in the European Community   *Geoffrey & Pippa Pridham*

3. European Integration, Regional Devolution and National Parliaments   *D. Coombes, L. Condorelli, R. Hrbek, W. Parsons, S. Schüttemeyer*

4. Eurocommunism and Foreign Policy   *Carole Webb*

Further studies scheduled for 1979/80

5. Liberalism in the European Community   *Ove Guldberg and Niels Haagerup*

6. Social Democracy in the European Community   *Norbert Gresch*

7. Political Forces in Spain, Greece and Portugal   *Beate Kohler*

8. The European Voter   *Jay Blumler and A. D. Fox*

Of related interest

Westminster and Devolution   *Study of Parliament Group in association with PSI*

I Introduction

The ranks of observers and analysts noting developments in the evolution of West European Communist parties have been swelled considerably as a result of what appeared, for a time, to be a tide of Communist electoral support which presented a major challenge to the political regimes in France and Italy. Eurocommunism, labelled and packaged by the media, contested and then absorbed by party spokesmen and more cautious academics, has spawned a wide range of questions, warnings and anticipations of future shifts in European domestic and international politics. Between 1975 and June 1979, the rise and fall in the electoral fortunes of the PCI (Partito Comunista Italiano), the PCF (Parti Communiste Français) and the PCE (Partido Comunista de España) stimulated widespread speculation on the possibilities and consequences of radical political change in Italy, France and Spain. The chances of Communist parties participating in West European government, albeit in coalition or in political circumstances likely to inhibit a sharp break with existing political and economic structures, has presented new opportunities for examining future political options, including the framework of international relations in Europe. What makes such a discussion both tantalising and intriguing is the debate over the existence or non-existence of Eurocommunism; in other words, the extent, sincerity and viability of the West European Communist parties' assertion of independence from the USSR and their commitment to a peaceful, parliamentary road to socialism.

Given the clear link between the adoption by the PCI, PCF and PCE of a so-called Eurocommunist platform in domestic and foreign policy and their expectation of electoral success, much of the analysis so far has centred on the tactical, as opposed to the strategic, significance of their apparent shift in attitudes, policies and objectives. Interest in the foreign policy consequences of Eurocommunism has been confined mainly to the short term, strongly influenced by speculation over the reactions of the USA and USSR to the participation in government of their erstwhile opponents and protegees.

Several electoral 'tests' provided one kind of measure by which the success and appeal of the three Communist parties' more nationally oriented strategies could be judged. The 'fall-out' from the two general elections in Italy in June 1976 and 1979, in Spain in June 1977 and March 1979 and the election in

1

France in March 1978 has shown some of the more optimistic estimates of changes to be misplaced and added to rather than resolved the uncertainty over the political direction of the Italian and French parties (see Table 1). In Italy, the PCI, having failed to win a majority in 1976, subsequently crept nearer to influencing government policy, initially by adopting a position of 'benevolent abstention' against the minority Christian Democratic Government, then moving into the official parliamentary majority in March 1978 on the basis of an agreed programme with the Andreotti Government. This programme fell short, however, of the full historic compromise which has been the PCI's major objective in its domestic political strategy, and, after uneasy relations with the Christian Democrats and a failure to achieve any Communist posts in government, the PCI withdrew its support in January, 1979. In the election which followed the PCI vote fell by 4 per cent from its 1976 total and the party decided to revert to its opposition role.

Table 1   Communist Party Electoral and Parliamentary Strength

		Per cent of vote	Number of Seats*
Partito Comunista Italiano	1976	34.4	227
	1979	30.4	201
European elections		29.6	24
Parti Communiste Français	1978	20.6	86
European elections		20.6	19
Partido Comunista de España	1977	9.5	19
	1979	10.7	23

* Seats in lower house

In Spain, by contrast, the PCE's relatively modest 9 per cent of the votes won in 1977, and its marginal increase to just over 10 per cent in the 1979 election, confirmed its electoral weakness relative to the Spanish Socialists and suggests that the PCE will not be in a position in the near future to exercise significant influence over the domestic and international choices facing Spain.

Any interim judgement on the electoral impact and success of Eurocommunism is made even more hazardous by the outcome of the French election. Not only did the Union of the Left fail to win, but the pre-election breakdown of relations between the PCF and its Socialist allies and the subsequent post-electoral recriminations between the two parties cast doubts on the commitment of the PCF to a common policy platform and an electoral alliance with the Socialist Party.

The measures of electoral success—or failure—imply that the threat or opportunity of Eurocommunism (depending on one's political inclinations and judgement) has now passed and with it the need to determine the shape and relevance of this rather elusive movement. Yet short term electoral considerations and assessments represent only one dimension of the debate on the changes in the strategies and objectives of West European Communist parties. In terms of foreign policy issues, moreover, they are not necessarily the most productive or interesting. Even without the prospect of immediate Communist participation in government, the Communist parties' electoral and parliamentary strength and impact on domestic politics pose some fundamental problems for the consensus, particularly the foreign policy consensus on which West European governments have hitherto based their policies.[1]

Since the second world war, West European Communist parties have been identified with fundamentalist opposition to the pro-American and especially pro-NATO orientation of West European foreign policies. Their domestic political isolation after 1947 and the international polarisation between the USA and USSR and their respective allies rendered West European Communist opposition ineffective or suspect. The tactical and policy changes associated with the emergence of Eurocommunism since the 1970s have combined to modify at least some of the critical postures of the PCI, PCF and PCE while bringing them closer to the centre of political influence. The outcome has been the development of a more constructive (though in many ways still ambiguous) critique of the foreign policy assumptions and priorities of West European governments which may be beginning to have some electoral and wider political impact. In these circumstances, interest in the foreign policies of the three major West European Communist parties turns partly on the identification of Eurocommunism with overt changes in foreign policy strategies and partly, and more generally, on the extent to which the structure and issues of international relations in Western Europe encourage or inhibit radical change in national foreign policies.

The focus of this short study, therefore, is twofold. Firstly, it sets out to redress the balance in discussions of Eurocommunism by exploring the specifically international and foreign policy dimensions of the parties' strategies and their evolution. While this external dimension cannot be divorced from internal organisational and ideological developments in the three parties, it does merit more detailed study than has been forthcoming hitherto. Secondly, the advent of more influential Communist parties in Western Europe, if not yet of Communist governments, raises both immediate and longer term issues for the foreign policies of West European states and the network of alliances and relationships which has emerged and grown more complex during the last two decades. The impact of the French and Italian

---

[1] It is worth noting that the PCI reached agreement with the Christian Democrats and four other parties in the Autumn of 1977 on a broad foreign policy programme which expressed their common adherence to the Atlantic and Western framework of Italian foreign policy and which appeared to survive the break-up of the parliamentary majority in the Spring of 1979.

Communist parties, in particular, on their countries' foreign policies should not be seen as confined entirely to their chances of securing places in government. Their attraction of votes and support are indicative of dissatisfaction with government performance and policies, some of which at least may be indirectly attributable to uncertainties and resentment stirred by apparently inadequate government responses to international economic crises and a fear of national claims being sacrificed to meet the needs of more powerful States and economic interests. It is also very striking that reaction to increased Communist influence, especially in France and Italy, has been as sharp and vociferous from outside these countries, from allies whose main preoccupation has been with the potential foreign policy consequences of domestic political shifts and anticipated political weakness and vulnerability.

In a yet wider sense, one of the major questions in intra-European relations, that of attitudes and expectations involved in Soviet/West European relations, is directly affected by the cross-currents of Communist party and inter-state contacts which have been disturbed by the greater assertiveness and electoral strength of the three West European Communist parties. Both analysis and a certain amount of speculation, therefore, are necessary in examining the significance of international issues to the phenomenon of Eurocommunism and the foreign policy reverberations resulting from more politically competitive and independent Communist parties in France, Italy and Spain.

A major feature of the re-examination of foreign policy positions by the PCI, PCF and PCE has been their awareness (albeit to a greater or lesser extent) of the existence of both opportunities and constraints stemming from the changes in the foreign policy environment of Western Europe. On the one hand, continuing detente and the anticipated decline in the relevance of the two politico-military blocs provide a more relaxed ideological and practical context within which specific national interests and priorities can be asserted. On the other hand, growing international economic interdependence has posed the problem starkly of the political and economic costs of a sharp reorientation in foreign policy and, even more clearly, has exposed the inevitable link between radical domestic reform and its external repercussions. The juxtaposition of these two themes in the foreign policy environment of Western Europe neatly reflects the fundamental tension which underlines the Communist parties' positions on foreign policy issues. For States in Western Europe, the financial, economic and strategic costs of striking out in an independent direction appear to be too great, even though national preoccupations and priorities seem to be diverging significantly from one another. For the Italian and French Communist parties, their challenge for a voice and influence in government has been made in domestic and international conditions which would appear effectively to constrain their ability to reshape drastically the direction and objectives of their countries' foreign policies. At the same time, their basic ideological commitment as Communist parties (in their belief in socialism as the successor to defeated capitalism and their reflex attachment to the Soviet Union) suggest foreign

4

policy goals and loyalties radically different from those embraced by existing governments. This study tries to reveal and illustrate the pressures and the often conflicting objectives which have combined to erode some of the traditional foreign policy tenets of the parties, while adding to the difficulty of forecasting their actions if they were to find themselves in positions to exercise influence in foreign policy.

The constraints imposed by the mantle of the Communist parties are of two kinds. The first stems from their historical, ideological and emotional involvement in an international communist movement which, in the past, has required West European Communist parties not to think in national or State terms but to give priority to a world revolutionary struggle and the interests of the first socialist State in the Soviet Union. Such a perspective has bequeathed a view of the world, and more recently of East-West conflict, markedly different from that of other political parties in Western Europe. Arguably, in spite of the parties' differences with the Soviet Union in the 1970s and their reshaping of their domestic images, this alternative outlook on foreign policy has proved more resistant to erosion by electorally-oriented strategies. The second set of constraints has more to do with the present and future context of Communist party political activities than with their historical ties. The parties' advocacy of a parliamentary road to power and the exploitation of alliances with other 'progressive forces' throws up a whole range of potential obstacles and limits to radical shifts in foreign policy and the assertion of international revolutionary loyalties which could trouble the consciences of the party members and detract from the credibility of their policies. It is not without interest, therefore, to note that the orchestrating of changes in foreign policy in all three parties has been seen as the task of the party leaderships, with an eye to the requirements of domestic political negotiation and the ideological and party importance of foreign policy issues.

The themes raised here are discussed at greater length, beginning in Chapter II with an exploration of the significance of international and foreign policy matters for the discussion of Eurocommunism. Chapter III examines the differences in the evolution of the French, Italian and Spanish Communist parties and also the different domestic contexts of their foreign policies essential for an understanding of their individual positions. Chapter IV deals specifically with foreign policy questions in relation to all three parties in the light of changes in the foreign policy environments at the national and international levels. Domestic international linkages are explored in Chapter V in terms of the parties' responses to the issues of international economic inter-dependence and membership and exploitation of the European Community.

II Foreign Policies and Eurocommunism

If there is scarcely any consensus of opinion on the actual existence or ultimate significance of Eurocommunism, there is substantial agreement on the issues and events that provide the battleground on which opposing sides have prepared their attack and defence. Eurocommunism has come to be seen as the product of a combination of international and domestic pressures which have pushed the PCI, PCF and PCE into asserting a more distinct national identity for themselves within the international Communist movement, and a more flexible and democratic image for their parties in their respective domestic political systems. These have been particularly evident from the early 1970s in the electoral advance of the three parties at the national level and, most publicly, in their gestures of defiance towards the USSR, culminating in the disagreements at the East Berlin summit of European Communist Parties in June 1976, and in the Madrid summit of March 1977 bringing together the three leaders, Georges Marchais of the PCF, Enrico Berlinguer of the PCI, and Santiago Carrillo of the PCE in an apparent affirmation of Western European solidarity.

It is probably unwise or even impossible to consider the relations between foreign policy questions and Eurocommunism without acknowledging further the contentious nature of the phenomenon itself.[1] Discussion of Eurocommunism is fraught with dangers and pitfalls, as the academic literature and the polemics of more closely involved political competitors and governments have shown. The attempt to establish the existence of a single and historically unique phenomenon of Eurocommunism has largely foundered in face of the visible differences among the Italian, French and Spanish Communist parties in their policies, domestic political situations and strategies and, above all, in their relations with the USSR. Hence, much of the analysis has been surrounded by a certain chimerical quality. This has been heightened by the difficulty of projecting into the future the impact on the political roles,

---

[1] For a cross-section of views and approaches to the topic of Eurocommunism see A. Kriegel, *Un autre communisme?,* Hachette, Paris, 1977; F. Claudin, *L'Eurocommunisme,* F. Maspero, Paris, 1977; J-F. Revel, 'The Myths of Eurocommunism', *Foreign Affairs,* January 1978; N. McInnes, *Eurocommunism,* Sage Washington Papers, 1977.

identity and viability of the three Communist parties of their apparent accommodation with certain aspects of parliamentary and 'bourgeois' democracy. In a forceful critique of Eurocommunism Jean-François Revel has argued that "Eurocommunism can be logical and coherent only if it results in the disappearance of Communism. This is the reason why its short history is already filled with illogicalities, contradictions and reversals."[2]

Another variant of the negative judgement on the bid for greater independence, democratic legitimacy and respectability on the part of the PCI, PCF and PCE has been the voicing of profound scepticism and suspicion concerning Communist party motives and the evidence of real and permanent change.[3] This assessment has been strongly influenced by the examination of Eurocommunism from a historical perspective. In particular, comparison has frequently been made between the broad alliance strategies and profession of commitment to political pluralism of the Communist parties in Eastern Europe in the late 1940s with the contemporary political tactics of the PCI, PCF and PCE. From this perspective, the emphasis in the critical scrutiny of Eurocommunism has lain in identifying the continuity of ideological commitment, the survival of the notion of the fundamental 'conquest of power', the paucity or purely cosmetic nature of changes in party organisation and the reservoir of instinctive loyalty of Communist party leaders and rank and file to the USSR. Allied to this scepticism has been the preference of many observers (including the USSR itself!) for suspending judgement on the existence or sincerity of Eurocommunism until the Communist parties actually enter government and reveal by their actions the extent of their criticisms of the Soviet model and their willingness to observe the rules of parliamentary democracy.

In spite of the volume of warnings, condemnation and reservations concerning the productiveness of Eurocommunist analysis, there have also been more positively-inclined studies. These have given rise to an interesting (and more open-ended) exploration of the domestic and international consequences of the independence and flexibility adopted by the Italian, French and Spanish Communist parties in their search for greater electoral appeal. For some, the public differences between these parties and the USSR and their refusal to accept unquestioningly the obligations and deference to the absolute solidarity of the international Communist movement, represent a decisive turning point in the development of international Communism; in particular, a shift in the manner of its organisation and the handling of relations between the Soviet Union and the more powerful Communist parties in the developed world.[4] On yet another level, attempts have been made to relate the domestic

---

[2] J-F. Revel, *op. cit.,* p. 305.

[3] See for example the views expressed by Dr. David Owen in the Hugh Anderson Memorial Lecture, 'Communism, Socialism and Democracy', Cambridge Union Society, 18 November, 1977.

[4] See discussion in L. Marcou and M. Riglet, 'Du passé font-ils table rase? La conférence de Berlin, Juin 1976', *Revue Française de Science Politique,* Vol. 26, No. 6, 1976 and L. Marcou in *Le Monde Diplomatique,* Mai, 1977.

and foreign policy changes of the PCI, PCF and PCE to the economic and political requirements of advanced, industrialised societies. Thus, the arguments which the Italian, Spanish and, to a lesser extent, the French Communist party leaderships have used in justification of their policy revisions have received some outside support.[5]

The spectrum of reactions to Eurocommunism is, then, very wide. Against this backcloth, discussion of foreign policy is doubly disadvantaged; firstly, because of the general doubts and differences of view referred to above and, secondly, because of the more specific features associated with the parties' handling of foreign policy in their domestic political strategies. Thus all three parties have, on the whole, given lower priority to foreign policy issues in their electoral campaigns between 1975 and 1978. It should, however, be noted that the PCI did devote some effort to publicising its position on NATO in the hope that this would increase the party's acceptability in the eyes of the Italian electorate.

The second aspect of the Communist parties' handling of foreign policy suggests that the parties have found it less 'costly' to modify their stances on foreign policy than on issues in the domestic arena. On a number of central points, they have found it possible to remain ambiguous, or to defer making important choices to the more distant future. Moreover, this ambiguity and deference to the contingent element in international politics has been difficult for the Communist parties' political competitors to challenge very precisely. This is particularly true of the future security system envisaged for Europe by the Communist parties, following the dissolution of the two blocs, and of foreign policy issues on which the attitudes of other countries (such as the USA) are vital but difficult to predict in detail in advance, (for example involvement in the NATO and EC frameworks). In other words, while it may be difficult to determine the real intentions of the parties on domestic policies, it is an even more hazardous and tenuous exercise in foreign policy.

In spite of these reservations it remains true in one important sense that foreign policy is central to Eurocommunism. West European Communist parties, with their intrinsic party links and identification with the Communist Party of the Soviet Union (CPSU), and a long standing ideological commitment to 'proletarian internationalism' and its association with the foreign policy objectives of the USSR, have been mistrusted, or in themselves ambivalent, concerning their status as truly 'national' parties. Their freedom to depart from their historic profile (in foreign policy terms) touches on the basic question of party cohesion and identity for their members and also *vis-à-vis* their party rivals in the political system. Thus, Donald Blackmer has argued in the case of the PCI, ''the more its domestic politics and programs come to resemble those of other groups, the more important it may be to continue to

---

[5] See especially R. Putnam, 'Interdependence and the Italian Communists', *International Organisation*, Spring, 1978.

offer a distinctly different international perspective and a different understanding of the nature and role of a political party."[6]

The foreign policy input into the debate on Eurocommunism will be examined in two ways. Firstly, it can be seen in terms of the *contextual* significance of international factors promoting opportunities and imposing constraints for the evolution of Communist party attitudes; secondly, as the *programmatic* contribution of foreign policy issues to the attempt by the three major parties to modify their domestic images and avoid the precipitation of external threats.

There has clearly been substantial agreement amongst analysts of Eurocommunism that whatever independence and criticism of the USSR has been attempted by the PCI, PCF and PCE has been sustained by, and has brought electoral rewards within the framework of, detente between the USA and USSR, and the consequent general relaxation of tension in European relations. Detente has somewhat damped down the inflammatory overtones of the Soviet connection and opened up debate at the national level on foreign policy objectives in which the Communist parties can profitably join. Thus, the domestic impact of detente has been to make parties like the PCF and PCI seem less of an absolute threat to basic national interests if they were ever to take part in government because there has appeared to be less need to make a stark choice between loyalty to 'East' or 'West' and loyalty to the party or the State. At the same time, it could be argued that detente has led to a coincidence of interests between the USSR and West European Communist parties in allowing both to exploit the improved atmosphere to make specific gains. While for the USSR these have included satisfaction of economic needs and recognition of the status quo in Europe, for the PCI and PCF, especially, they have involved greater opportunities for electoral alliances, where necessary, with Socialist and Catholic parties, and even the expansion of their own electoral base which had hitherto been limited by the polarisation of the cold war.

Furthermore, in a more indirect fashion, detente has led to greater scrutiny of the demands made by alliance membership in Western Europe including defence expenditure, adherence to American foreign policy priorities and a more critical assessment of the contribution made by the existing military blocs to peace and security in Europe. In both Italy and France, such discussion no longer finds the Communist parties quite so isolated or suspect.

Even so the contribution of detente has not been solely positive. Precisely because it has enabled the USSR to exploit its purely national or State interests, it has stretched to the limit the patience and political skills of some European Communist party leaders at a time when modification of their own revolutionary posture has put strains on party cohesion. Thus, in 1974, the PCF's attempts to develop a broad alliance in opposition to the allegedly pro-

6 D. Blackmer, 'Continuity and Change in Postwar Italian Communism', in D. Blackmer and S. Tarrow (eds.), *Communism in Italy and France,* Princeton University Press, 1975, p. 67.

Atlanticist Presidency of Giscard d'Estaing, were somewhat confounded by the evident satisfaction of the USSR at Giscard d'Estaing's election and Soviet hopes for still further improvement in Franco-Soviet relations.[7]

The second feature of the international context which has been linked to changes in both the domestic and foreign policy priorities of the PCI, PCF and PCE is more controversial. One of the more ambitious attempts to find an explanation for part of the political and economic 'reformism' of Eurocommunism has been the suggestion that processes of international economic interdependence in Western Europe have reached a point where radical reversals in foreign policy are effectively excluded.[8] While detente has promoted political opportunism in foreign policy, international economic interdependence is seen to have constrained the formulation of socialist economic policies, hitherto inspired by the need to reduce participation in the framework of Western political economy. Thus, the domestic and international economic policies of the PCI and PCE (both characterised by concessions to private economic factors) appear increasingly to stress the need to preserve the link between their economies and the outside world, including acknowledgement of at least a partially regulatory role for the European Community.[9] The implications of international economic interdependence are said to exercise not only a direct economic but also a more general political constraint. One of the preoccupations which has emerged in the domestic political strategy of the PCI and PCE since 1973 and, to a lesser extent in that of the PCF, has been concern for the political vulnerability of newly-established left-wing governments. The fear has been widely expressed that external creditors of these governments might anticipate future decisions and prematurely withdraw their support without giving a left-wing government the opportunity to establish itself and its credentials.

Compared with the influence of detente, the impact of interdependence on the calculations of the Italian, Spanish and French Communist parties is much less easy to determine in a precise or uniform way. There are noticeable differences, for example, in the extent to which deference to the rhetoric of interdependence is made in official analyses of the freedom of States to pursue autonomous policies. Giorgio Amendola, admittedly one of the PCI's most committed exponents of this view has argued: 'Today the national sovereignty of every country is already limited in fact. That is a consequence of economic interdependence, of the need for loans, of the development of multinational firms, of every sort of bond, apart from political conditions tied to the existence of military blocs. One must give up the idea that there is a national,

---

[7] See discussion on this point in N. McInnes, *The Communist Parties of Western Europe,* Oxford University Press, 1975.

[8] This is the argument developed in R. Putnam, *op. cit.*

[9] See Chapter V. Also for discussion of PCI and its changing economic interpretation of the EC, see D. Sassoon, 'Introduction: The European Strategy of the Italian Communist Party' in D. Sassoon (ed.), *The Italian Communists Speak for Themselves,* Spokesman, European Socialist Thought Series, No. 11, 1978.

sovereign state that can decide its own fate in full autonomy. That is an anachronistic idea.'[10]

The PCF, by contrast, takes every opportunity to stress the paramount importance and feasibility of national independence. In addition, an awareness of the limitations imposed by interdependence on national foreign and domestic policy appears to be selective, even on the part of the PCI, in the sense that only certain international arenas are acceptable. If taken too far, the logic of the interdependence argument deprives Communist, or indeed radical socialist parties of any room to alter significantly the political and economic direction of their societies. While the PCI and PCE have appeared to take more seriously the risk of external threats to radical governments, they are far from conceding that the construction of their model of socialism is inconceivable in advanced industrialised countries.

The other ambiguous factor in the recognition by the PCI, PCF and PCE of the intensified economic interdependence of West European states is their identification of its mechanisms and rationale with American and German hegemony. Both the PCI and PCF originally opposed the European Community as an organisation likely to strengthen American economic penetration of Western Europe and provide conditions for the extension of monopoly capitalism. Although both parties have subsequently modified their attitudes towards the European Community, their determination to end what they have seen as the subservience of national economies to the priorities of international capitalism remains a prominent feature of their proposals for a socialist alternative to the handling of domestic economic policy.

Clearly the overriding factor in the international context which has shaped the evolution of the PCI, PCF and PCE over the last five years has been their relationship with the USSR. In almost every cross-examination of the significance of Eurocommunism the role of the Soviet Union has been emphasised, either as the catalyst of change or as the continuing, underlying link which prevents any change in policy or attitude from being taken seriously. The most important aspects of relations between the USSR and the three major West European Communist parties have been ideological and organisational cohesion within the international Communist movement, specific criticisms directed against the USSR itself, and the pressures on the PCI, PCF and PCE to modify their pro-Soviet image to achieve greater electoral success within their own countries. While differences in these areas have been substantial and, in some cases, like that of Carrillo's comprehensive attack on the USSR, publicly declared, individual foreign policy problems have not figured prominently as contentious ideological or tactical issues. Thus, the USSR's role has been much more important on the party-to-party level than as a result of its particular national foreign policy orientation.

There are, however, two exceptions, although neither have been pushed far

---

[10] 'Intervista con Giorgio Amendola', Appendix to G. Luciani, *Il PCI e il Capitalismo Occidentale,* Milan, Longanesi, 1977, quoted in R. Putnam, *op. cit.,* p. 318.

enough yet by any of the three parties to the point of a crisis in their relations with the USSR. The first difference of opinion (that of the correct interpretation of detente), has tended, ironically in the light of the 'reformist' tendencies of Eurocommunism, to instil doubts in the minds of some French, Italian and Spanish Communist leaders about the Soviet Union's commitment to fundamental political change. Misgivings over the USSR's interests in detente have already been referred to in the PCF's discomfort at having its political opposition to Giscard d'Estaing overturned by the USSR's appreciation of the French Centre-Right government's interest in giving prominence to bilateral economic and political relations with the Soviet Union. These misgivings have been aired in a more general way by the PCI and PCE. Both parties have voiced their suspicions that the priority given to detente and peaceful coexistence implies the endorsement of an international equilibrium, which itself ignores contradictions and pressures for change in both capitalist and Socialist societies. From the perspective of the Italian and Spanish parties, far removed from the pressures on the super powers, opportunities for exploiting contradictions are not to be sacrificed for global diplomatic goals.[11]

The second foreign policy difference *vis-à-vis* the USSR posits the link between the commitment to democratic political principles in the construction of socialism domestically and their assertion in foreign policy. Increasingly since the condemnation of the Warsaw Pact invasion of Czechoslovakia (and recalling the PCF's earlier condemnation of the Soviet trials of Daniel and Siniavsky in 1966), all three parties have openly criticised the Soviet and East European treatment of dissidents. On occasions, the PCI and PCF have publicly endorsed the positions of individuals and protest groups in Poland and Czechoslovakia and argued in favour of cultural and intellectual freedom as being entirely consistent with a socialist society.[12] Such criticisms and assertions have been principally a part of the ideological debate between the USSR and West European Communist parties on the relationship between democracy and socialism. Nevertheless, they have spilled over into foreign policy as a result of the prominence given to human rights in Basket Three of the CSCE's Helsinki Declaration and in the differences separating the USSR from Western European governments on the issue at the Belgrade follow-up conference. The Soviet, Czechoslovakian and Polish dissident groups have used the Helsinki framework to strengthen their cases against their governments and have still been supported by the PCI, PCF and PCE. This is a judgement which must turn very much on the actual observance and priority of the Helsinki human right principles in the foreign policy of a future Left government in France or Italy, especially when linked to other pressures to adopt a more sympathetic view of the Soviet Union's 'peaceful intentions' in European relations. Nevertheless it does appear that the PCI, PCF and PCE

---

11 L. Marcou and M. Riglet, *op. cit.*, p. 1072.
12 *L'Humanité*, December 13 and 16, 1977.

hold a rather wider interpretation of the Helsinki commitments than does the USSR.

Most observers have focussed on the domestic rather than the international context in Italy, France and Spain in their search for explanations of the political conditions for the emergence of Eurocommunism. The originality and convergence in the domestic political strategies of the PCI, PCF and PCE have been viewed (positively) as a creative response to the dilemma of securing overdue political, economic and social change in societies where political opposition has been weakened by divisions; or (negatively) as a disguised take-over of democratic institutions as a prelude to the imposition of a Communist dictatorship. In other words, domestic political acceptability and credibility have been the prime twin concerns of the parties themselves and their assessors. Foreign policy issues have not been excluded from this search for greater electoral and wider political appeal. Their programmatic usefulness to the three parties can be traced to the three major areas where the declared commitment to a 'peaceful road to socialism' has had an impact on domestic politics; the enhancement of the democratic legitimacy of the Communist parties themselves, the conclusion of political alliances for electoral and government purposes and deference to 'national realities', especially perceived in economic and security terms.

From this perspective some foreign policy questions have clearly been more appropriate and salient than others. In terms of the similarities between the parties, those foreign policy issues which have surfaced in domestic debate can be summarised and grouped as follows. In the case of each group more detailed discussion will follow in the next three chapters and only brief reference will be made at this point to individual party positions.

The first group consists of two principal issues, NATO and the European Community. In France and Italy they have traditionally been regarded as central pivots of national foreign policy and therefore as determining factors in the electoral identification of political parties. In Italy both have been seen as 'test cases' of support for internal liberal democracy as well as a willingness to accept existing international obligations and an acknowledgment of Italy's dependence on external links for vital economic and security resources.[13] In France, neither NATO nor the European Community have been presented quite so emphatically as 'test cases' because of more persistent and widespread reservations across the political spectrum concerning their correspondence with French interests and sensitivities. Nevertheless, the PCF's opposition to both organisations has been interpreted, by the advocates of NATO and the EC, as being far more dangerous than, for example, that of the Gaullists, with whom it has been frequently linked, because of the PCF's external involvement with the Soviet Union. Between 1972 and 1977 the PCF and PCI moved from outright opposition to any form of involvement with NATO

---

[13] For full discussion of this argument see P. Vannicelli, *Italy, NATO and the European Community,* Harvard Studies in International Affairs, No. 31, Harvard University, 1974.

(regarding it as both anti-Soviet and prejudicial to overall European security), to a rather indeterminate commitment, in the event of their coming to power, neither to end nor to intensify the existing links between their countries and NATO. This commitment has been rationalised more thoroughly and enthusiastically by the PCI compared with the PCF, in terms of the need not to provoke a sudden shift in the politico-military equilibrium in Europe by a unilateral withdrawal from NATO which would be unlikely to be reciprocated by the Warsaw Pact. The issue of NATO has not held the same significance for the PCE since Spain is not a member of NATO. Given the relative isolation of Spain under Franco from the framework of Western European security, NATO has not had a comparable symbolic significance as the benchmark of party acceptability in foreign policy terms. Without any positive move within Spain to promote active consideration of Spanish membership of NATO, the PCE's own opposition to NATO has not led to its domestic isolation on this question. The party has, on the other hand, sought to mollify the fears of more conservative political opinion and thereby extend its national appeal by committing itself to not requiring the removal of American bases from Spain if it were to enter government.

By contrast, membership of the European Community has been turned into a much more positive campaigning issue by the PCI and PCE, if not the PCF, in spite of earlier opposition as resolute as that to the NATO alliance. The PCE, far from being constrained by ideological inhibitions or party competition with the Partido Socialista Obrero Español (Spanish Socialist Workers Party) has enthusiastically supported Spanish entry into the Community, beyond the point of minimal toleration made necessary by purely electoral demands. The PCI has taken longer to re-evaluate the broad question of European integration in terms of its domestic and international significance for Italy compared with the PCF whose accommodation to the Community in 1972 within the framework of the Common Programme had all the signs of a very reluctant and circumscribed concession in response to short-term political priorities.[14]

A second group of foreign policy issues arising out of the domestic strategy of the PCI and PCF, in particular, covers those which have been contentious in political alliance negotiations. Here a distinction needs to be made between the more intensive and detailed policy discussions over the Common Programme in 1972 and 1976-77 among the PCF and its partners in the Union of the Left, the French Socialist Party and the Left Radicals, and the more limited considerations of the PCI in anticipation of a future coalition role with the Italian Christian Democrats. In the latter case, the close identification of the Christian Democrats with both the European Community and NATO has turned these into questions on which the PCI has sought some recognition of

---

[14] For comparisons of PCF and PCI attitudes on the European Community see R. Irving, 'The European Policy of the French and Italian Communists', *International Affairs,* Vol. 53, No. 3, July 1977.

its change of attitude as a means of bridging the ideological and policy gulf between the two parties. Within the French Union of the Left and in spite of the fact that foreign policy differences were played down both in the 1971-72 and 1976-77 negotiations, two issues, the maintenance of the 'force de frappe' and direct elections to the European Parliament, emerged in 1977 as highly contentious questions. They revealed the conflicting pressures and assumptions not far below the surface which would have caused serious difficulties had the Union of the Left succeeded in winning the elections. The PCF's limited endorsement of the 'force de frappe' and its decision not to oppose direct elections to the European Parliament were both examples of the characteristic handling of such divisive issues within the political alliance negotiations. Both involved the PCF in unilateral policy reversals thereby imposing pressures on its coalition partners to make similar concessions on other matters.[15]

The third group of foreign policy issues comprises questions which have not so far been subject to any substantial change, or even limited and defensive modification, by the Communist parties in response to the critical attitudes of other parties. Thus, many observers have noted the range of foreign policy questions on which the PCI, PCF and PCE have continued to support the Soviet view and on which the parties have judged there would be less to gain from provoking a conflict with the USSR or from stretching internal party bonds to breaking point. These include the continuing unfavourable comparison between the hegemonical tendencies of the USA and the basically peaceful profile of the USSR within the framework of European relations, support for the Soviet position on the danger of imperialism in the Third World, especially the distinctions made between Western and socialist 'intervention' or 'assistance' in Africa and, finally, hostility to Israel in the Middle East.

Two points can be noted from this preliminary identification and summary of the foreign policy issues which have been most prominent in the domestic political campaign arena of the PCI, PCF and PCE. Firstly, the number and type of issues have been limited by the ease with which the parties could hope to make electoral gains and defuse the suspicion of potential allies, without totally jeopardising their internal cohesion and their underlying sympathy with the USSR's analysis of the major features of international politics. This has required some political dexterity and an ability on the part of the party leaderships to control the consequences of reversals on foreign policy issues. Secondly, although there has been some common ground on the issues on which all three parties have shifted their positions, there remains, nevertheless, significant variation in the degree to which foreign policy has been exploited in the interests of political legitimacy. This is linked, in part, to differences amongst the parties in relation to the whole framework and strategy of

---

[15] See also discussion in Chapters III and IV.

15

promoting 'national roads to socialism', in part also to more fundamental variations in general domestic responses to foreign policy issues in each of the three countries. These will be explored further in the next chapter.

There is one further aspect of the discussion concerning the external activities of the PCF, PCI and PCE which has a potential bearing on their foreign policy attitudes both *vis-à-vis* one another's priorities and in relation to the USSR. The appearance of a West European 'regional bloc' within the international Communist movement has been one of the principal bones of contention in the evaluation of French, Italian and Spanish criticisms of the USSR and the means by which these criticisms have been developed. Signs of a convergence of views and tactics associated with an emphasis on distinctive West European political traditions and values emerged in the various joint statements and communiques from meetings involving PCI, PCF and PCE leaders and officials between 1975 and 1977. These were strengthened by the appearance of solidarity given by the three parties during the East Berlin Conference of European Communist parties in June, 1976. A full discussion of the implications of these disputes within the international Communist movement during this period lies outside the scope of this study.[16] Nevertheless, two aspects of the debate concerning the West European regional dimension of Eurocommunism are relevant.

The identification of a distinct 'regional bloc' turns partly on assessments of the nature of the differences between the three major West European Communist Parties and the USSR, and partly on their readiness to give their positions some formal, organisational shape. One of the factors encouraging speculation on the possibility of a rift within the international Communist movement was the increase in bilateral and multilateral contact between the PCI, PCF and PCE, the publicity given to these meetings and the willingness of the parties to express their views in joint communiqués. Thus a series of bilateral meetings took place both before and after the East Berlin Conference, the most important bringing together the PCF and PCE in July and the PCI and PCF in November, 1975.

In the period preceding the elections in Spain and France contacts intensified, culminating in the tripartite summit of the three leaders in Madrid in March, 1977 (coinciding with a meeting of the East European Communist parties in Sofia) and a top-level meeting between Berlinguer and Marchais in May, 1977. It would be misleading, however, to see in these inter-party contacts the beginnings of a new bloc or even a regional caucus. Not only has the format of the Madrid summit not been repeated but, more significantly, Berlinguer, Marchais and Carrillo have constantly denied any intention of creating a regional grouping within, still less in opposition to, the international Communist movement. Indeed, PCI spokesmen have stressed that a bloc mentality is precisely what they oppose both in international relations and in

---

16 See further L. Marcou and M. Riglet, *op. cit.*

the handling of relations between Communist parties. Although no overall or permanent organisational link has been established as a result of these meetings, the PCF and PCI did agree to establish a 'mixed commission', following their May 1977 meeting, to generate a series of discussions among senior party officials and parliamentarians on policy problems covering a range of sectors relevant to Franco-Italian relations.[17] It is difficult at this stage to determine the impact of these rather specialised policy discussions on the wider question of the attitudes of the two parties to their individual and joint relations with the rest of the international Communist movement. One might suggest that despite the generally harmonious picture presented in official reports of the first two meetings of the 'mixed commission', the second being devoted to European Community issues, the two delegations could not have found it easy to reconcile their own mutual differences on a number of concrete policy questions.

From a short-term perspective the proliferation of meetings and contacts during this period between the PCI, PCF and PCE could be interpreted more reasonably as evidence of the concern of the PCE to improve and extend its international image as part of its campaign for legalisation, and the expectation of the French and Italian parties that collective declarations of support for a democratic path to socialism would bring domestic electoral rewards.

The foreign policy implications of the apparent convergence in the views and tactics of the French, Italian and Spanish Communist parties are difficult to determine, not least because the three parties did not give much prominence to external questions in their joint meetings.[18] On those issues where the three have deviated from the USSR line, the timing and extent of their policy changes have varied in accordance with internal party and separate domestic pressures. On the other hand, it could be argued that the assertion of distinctive, West European democratic traditions domestically does have an external equivalent in the emphasis which the PCE and PCI, especially, have given to the need to promote the particular interests of Western Europe in the international system. This has led the PCI to campaign against what it sees as Western Europe's 'marginalisation' in the decision-making processes involving economic and security questions of central importance to individual States and the region as a whole. Clearly the strongest stimulus to this definition of a regional identity is anti-Americanism. Indeed, negative repudiation of American influence and penetration has been much more pronounced than any positive agreement on the precise objectives or

---

[17] Communique of commission meeting dealing with European Community issues, May 26, 1978, published in *Les Communistes Français et l'Europe,* No. 2, June 1978, pp. 24-25 (produced by PCF delegation to the European Parliament).

[18] The communique from the Berlinguer-Marchais meeting on May 3, 1977 did include references to the need for co-operation with 'democratic socialist and christian forces' in France, Italy and the whole of Western Europe to promote detente and disarmament and the need by all signatories to implement the principles of the Helsinki Final Act.

organisational framework which would be appropriate in the pursuit of greater West European independence.

A corollary of the definition of a regional dimension to West European foreign policy is the acceptance that effective national foreign policies both rely on, and should contribute towards, the consolidation of resources and co-ordination of views at the European level. However, even in declaratory terms, deference to the significance of the European dimension is not shared equally by the PCI, PCF and PCE, either in relation to existing European institutions or in anticipation of some future co-operative framework. As will be shown in greater detail later, different party traditions and evaluations of national circumstances have combined to make the PCE and PCI more willing and likely to acknowledge the relevance of regional links, while the PCF has sought to reduce these to a minimum. Thus, in organisational and external policy terms, evidence of a self-conscious, regionally-oriented strategy supported by all three parties is both tenuous and ambiguous.

The objective of this chapter has not been to resolve the multiplicity of uncertainties and conflicting views which have dogged the discussion of Eurocommunism. Rather the intention has been to isolate and briefly to assess the contribution of foreign policy questions to the attempts of the PCI, PCF and PCE to strengthen their domestic base and make a bid for power. It would not be appropriate to argue from the foregoing analysis that the international context to which the domestic strategies of the PCI, PCF and PCE have in part been a response, has been the crucial factor in stimulating a re-orientation of the parties' objectives and tactics. Nor would it be accurate to suggest further that foreign policy issues were, or continue to be, vital in increasing votes or losing support in elections. What is clear is that a fully satisfactory explanation of the changed preoccupations of the PCI, PCF and PCE in relation to their short, if not their long-term, goals cannot ignore the interrelationship between domestic and foreign policy.

III National Contexts and Strategies

The debate on Eurocommunism has been characterised by an underlying tension. This has shown itself in the preferences of some observers for pinpointing similarities in the international assertiveness and domestic image-building of the PCI, PCF and PCE, while others have insisted on uncovering national differences which they regard as central to any evaluation of the political impact of these parties. The relative weight which is given to uniformity or diversity depends on one's focus and purpose in examining the undercurrents of change in the Communist parties of Western Europe. Those who have approached Eurocommunism with some scepticism or with an eye to the combination of personalities and the historical experiences of the parties both within their national political systems and as exiles from them, have seen in the national situation of each of the major parties signs of constraining circumstances, which have conditioned their progress towards accommodation with 'political realities'. One of the challenges in the interpretation of the shifts made by the PCI, PCF and PCE lies in making the link between internal party evolution and the developments in the wider national political and policy arena which have apparently persuaded the party leaderships, if not the rank and file, of the need to revise their strategies. From this point of view an assessment of the motives, extent and success of the foreign policy modifications undertaken by the three parties demands some exploration of their national contexts.

Variations in the 'National Roads to Socialism'

The reassessment of their foreign policy positions by the PCI, PCF and PCE can be seen either as the consequence of a fundamental reorientation of each party, the product of increasing criticism of the USSR and pressures producing closer integration into their national political systems; or purely as part of a tactical plan to help remove obstacles in the path to power, after which 'revisionism' and assertions of independence may be quickly repudiated. These sharply opposed interpretations reflect different basic assumptions and analyses of past and future events which make them appear incapable of being conclusively resolved. Moreover, neither does justice to the range of cross cutting pressures impelling each party towards extending the margin of independence from the USSR whilst seeking to avoid the ultimate cost to party and wider Communist solidarity of an actual rupture of relations in the political or ideological sphere. Such pressures have been felt to a greater or lesser extent and produced some significant variations in responses among the three parties.

The following brief summaries of the particular factors influential in the reshaping of each party's overall political approach emphasise the interaction of two major sorts of changes in the international and domestic environments which have affected the orthodox reflexes of the parties. The first has been the weakening of the Soviet Union's pre-eminent role within the international Communist movement, in the more recent period marked by the dissension sparked off by de-Stalinisation and the issues and party splits raised by the Sino-Soviet schism. These dented a severe chink, albeit one scarcely exploited very far at the time, in the pristine armour of the CPSU as the leading Communist party. The armour was penetrated more dramatically as a result of the USSR's handling of the Czech reform movement and drastic resort to invasion to restore Soviet control. The Czechoslovakian invasion did not at the time, or indeed subsequently, provoke a total break with the USSR. However, it was primarily responsible for opening up the doubts which eventually led to West European Communist parties becoming increasingly wary of the dangers of subscribing to the monolithic image of the international Communist movement. The sense of international identity, previously paramount, had been punctured.

Secondly, it became clear by the early 1970s that opportunities in the domestic political arenas of France and Italy (somewhat later in Spain) suggested a means by which the Communist parties could emerge from their relative political isolation and make a serious bid for power, so ending the frustration of maintaining a revolutionary posture in a protracted non-revolutionary political context. Seizing the opportunities, however, required appropriate gestures and responses to sustain the willingness of previously hostile competitors on the Left to pool resources in order to create a substantial and winning electoral coalition; or, in Italy and Spain, to establish more basic credentials as legitimate and essential participants in a broad political movement to find solutions for a profound national crisis.

The Partito Comunista Italiano (PCI)

The reputation and credentials of the PCI as the source and inspiration of the 'Eurocommunism movement' have been widely, if sometimes inaccurately noted. The party's own intellectual history and in particular, Togliatti's[1] analysis of Italy's postwar domestic and international political situation (though not without initial setbacks and contradictions), pointed to the

---

[1] Palmiro Togliatti, party leader from 1937 to 1964 and the PCI's architect of its immediate post-war strategy.

evolution of a domestic strategy capable of adjusting the PCI's role to the structures and processes of advanced industrial democracies. Overlooking the party's misconceived expectations of its indispensability to Italy's postwar political reconstruction, it is possible to detect an underlying continuity in Togliatti's view of the PCI role in 1944 and Berlinguer's conception of party strategy from 1973 onwards. As P. Allum has commented of the earlier period:

> 'Its implications (i.e. the PCI's participation in the Resistance) which are important for the party's subsequent activity, were that the party saw the role of the working class in Italian society more in liberal democratic than in classical Marxist terms; consequently, the PCI's identification with the national interest meant that it selected its demands on the basis of the national interest as it viewed it, rather than claim that the national interest coincide with its sectional demands.'[2]

The Gramscian heritage [3] of the PCI reconciled the party's readiness to work within the basic structures of Italian society, with its revolutionary goals and character, by viewing the conquest of power as the gradual assertion of working class 'hegemony' throughout the various parts of Italian 'civil society'. The combination of a professed national commitment and an awareness of the obstacles inhibiting the application of Leninist tactics to the pursuit of revolutionary change has been seen as one of the principal features of 'la via italiana al socialismo'. Another major feature concerns the relations between the PCI and the international Communist movement which have shaped the party's external image.[4] This has identified the PCI, not merely as a party unafraid to express criticism of the USSR, but more broadly, as the proponent of toleration and diversity within the Communist movement as a whole. It has been tempting to see in the evolution[5] of the PCI's position, a gradual but cumulative undermining of its relations with the USSR. Yet it is as well to remember that the PCI has never reached the point of provoking a complete rupture. As a party it has not been prepared to take the ultimate step of denying the socialist character of the Soviet Union. Indeed, contacts between PCI leaders and officials and the CPSU have been notable for their friendliness and regularity over the last five years compared, for example, with those of the PCF whose identification with the USSR has in the past seemed much more solid.

---

[2] P. Allum, *The Italian Communist Party Since 1945,* Occasional Paper, No. 2, University of Reading, Graduate School of Contemporary European Studies, 1970, p. 7.

[3] Antonio Gramsci, a founding member and leader of the PCI from 1923 to 1937 and the party's leading ideologist.

[4] For major studies of this aspect see D. Blackmer, *Unity in Diversity: Italian Communism and the Communist World,* MIT Press, 1968, and D. Blackmer and A. Kriegel, *The International Role of the Communist Parties in Italy and France,* Harvard Studies in International Affairs, No. 33, Harvard, 1974.

[5] From Togliatti's critical reaction to the revelations of the CPSU's Twentieth Congress and his advocacy of the principles of autonomy and polycentrism in 1964, to the refusal to endorse the method or justification for the Czechoslovak invasion and Berlinguer's persistently independent posture.

It is arguable that the balancing act which the PCI has sought to maintain with the USSR and its exploration of the possibilities and justifications for accepting diversity within the international Communist movement stem from attempts to marry a range of conflicting attitudes and pressures. A fundamental issue has been the USSR's claim to ideological and 'managerial' ascendancy over both ruling and non-ruling Communist parties, which has concerned the PCI since Togliatti, because of the possible consequences both for the party's own domestic political future and for international relations in Europe. By 1968, the PCI's international defence of the right to autonomy for individual parties (including the Chinese) and the emphasis it placed on the need to phase out the two politico-military blocs underlined the central role which 'the terrain for autonomous political development' had come to play in the party's long term strategy.[6]

Between 1968 and 1974 this was given a further twist in the PCI's condemnation and continuing criticism of the Soviet-led Warsaw Pact invasion of Czechoslovakia. The party argued forcefully that the Czech political developments did not constitute a fundamental threat to socialism, still less to Soviet security, and therefore did not warrant interference with the Czechoslovakian Communist party. It further contended that the invasion confirmed the dangers incipient in 'the logic of the blocs', thus challenging the USSR's own view of the limits (or rather lack of them) to its influence within the socialist camp. The USSR's invocation of the Brezhnev Doctrine[7] was seen by the PCI as an unacceptable blurring of ideological conformity with the dubious notions of enforcing political stability and socialist security.

The preoccupation of the PCI, more recently, has been with advancing justifications for its resistance to attempts by the USSR to mobilise the international movement in line with its own priorities in 1976 and 1977. Clearly reflecting the party's concentration on issues in its national political campaign, Berlinguer championed, at the Berlin Conference of Communist parties, the right of West European parties, in particular, to develop their socialist strategies within a framework of respect for pluralism and individual freedoms. The PCI's continuing resistance to Soviet assertiveness was amply demonstrated by its active participation in the moves before and during the conference to refute the USSR's conception of the meeting as an endorsement of the Communist movement's internal unity.[8] Unlike the PCF, the PCI had no doubts about expressing the fundamental external loyalties of Communist parties in terms of 'voluntary international solidarity' rather than 'proletarian

---

[6] For discussion of this theme, see D. Sassoon, 'Introduction: The European Strategy of the Italian Communist Party' in D. Sassoon (ed.), *The Italian Communists Speak for Themselves*, Spokesman, European Socialist Thought Series, No. 11, 1978.

[7] This refers to the argument put forward by Brezhnev, leader of the Soviet Communist Party, justifying his country's invasion of Czechoslovakia on the grounds that intervention by a socialist State in defence of another socialist regime constituted legitimate infringement of the latter's sovereignty.

[8] On this point see K. Devlin, 'The Challenge of Eurocommunism' in *Problems of Communism*, Vol. XXVI, Jan-Feb. 1977.

internationalism'. It saw in the former, an opportunity to counter the 'unilateralist' interpretation of internationalism as unquestioned support for the Soviet Union with a less all-embracing commitment that did not invariably associate criticism of the USSR with anticommunism.

The independent profile of the PCI has not, of course, stemmed only from its conflicts with the USSR within the international Communist movement. The party's domestic political activities have contributed as much, if not more, to its distinctive character. These can be summed up as the attempt by the PCI over a long period to combine revolutionary purpose with the establishment of its presence throughout Italian society, at national, regional and local levels, in the hope of achieving fundamental transformation through the democratic process. The 'gradualist' option led to the PCI, by the early 1970s, adopting a cooperative stance in parliamentary activities in spite of its formal status in the opposition, and to the party's active involvement in local administration both as a majority party and in alliance with other political forces. The second motive behind the PCI's long term domestic strategy involved the extension of the party's electoral and membership base beyond the 'proletariat,' to embrace even those previously deterred by the party's association with anticlericalism and to attract support from white collar and small business groups, in a bid to project the PCI as a genuine mass party and to overcome its political isolation.[9]

The most overt and comprehensive expression of the party's commitment to modifying its confrontational role in Italian politics, and its major preoccupation since 1973, has been the strategy of the 'historic compromise'. The wisdom, feasibility and survival capacity of the 'historic compromise' have been extensively debated inside and outside the party.[10] In the place of a numerical victory for the Left at the polls to secure political change in Italy, the strategy envisages a long term coalition among the three major parties, the Christian Democrats, Communists and Socialists, but with the emphasis clearly on the importance of collaboration between the first two. On the one hand, it offered a possible solution to the failure to deal effectively with Italy's political problems in the wake of continuous decline in the authority and effectiveness of the Christian Democrats and the collapse of the Centre Left alliance with the Socialists. On the other, the PCI saw it as an opportunity to maximise the political leverage from its steady but not, by 1973, overwhelming electoral advance and a means by which it could disarm its internal and external opponents.

The PCI's adherence to the 'compromesso storico' has had a marked impact in determining its internal and external priorities both before and after the

---

[9] For discussion of development of PCI strategy see P. Allum, *op. cit.;* M. Padovani, *La Longue Marche: Le PCI,* Calman-Levy, Paris, 1976; S. Tarrow, 'Communism in Italy and France: Adaptation and Change' in S. Tarrow and D. Blackmer *Communism in Italy and France,* Princeton UP, 1975.

[10] For a critical view from the outside see P. Allum, 'La crise structurelle et politique du PCI', *Le Monde Diplomatique,* July 1978.

1976 elections. Between 1973 and the election of June 1976, a major campaign on both the domestic and international fronts was undertaken to reinforce the party's credibility and appeal as a vital participant in a future grand alliance. This involved some specific changes or toning down in policies and attitudes as well as displays of responsible political campaigning as in the divorce referendum in 1974. Arguably, although the June election was in some ways regarded as too premature by the party leadership to allow the PCI to reap the maximum benefit from its canvassing of broader support, the division of votes between the Christian Democratic Party and the PCI at the expense of the smaller parties including the Socialists, produced a parliamentary situation not too far removed from that anticipated by the most hopeful proponents of the 'historic compromise'.

Since the election, the Christian Democrats' need of further support to maintain their government in office, and the refusal of the Socialist party to offer any support without the involvement of the Communists, has effectively required PCI participation in the majority. The PCI has moved, in two years, from positive abstention to entering finally the parliamentary majority, though not the government, on the basis of an agreement on a limited policy programme with the Andreotti Government and open involvement of the PCI in the formation of policy. After a number of differences over policies and especially the issue of Communist participation in the Cabinet, the PCI finally withdrew its support from the Andreotti Government in January, 1979. Its probable return into opposition following its slight loss of seats in the June 1979 election will at least give the party leadership an opportunity to reflect on the experiences of its experimentation with the strategy of limited accommodation with the traditional enemy.

Perhaps the most striking feature so far of the PCI's planting of a foot over the threshold is not so much the impact on government style or policy substance, as the evident costs and strains to the party itself. The very conditions envisaged for the realisation of the 'historic compromise'—a national crisis and need for reconciliation of opposing conceptions of change—have exposed the PCI leadership and parliamentary group to rank and file criticism, if not electoral losses, and resentment from those economic groups whose interests the party has embraced.[11] This brings the discussion back to the point made earlier. The PCI's exploration of the margin for safe and necessary manoeuvre internationally has been pushed even further in its calculations of the steps considered essential for achieving political power securely (and not, under Italian conditions, just temporarily), at home.

The Parti Communiste Français (PCF)
Most observers have not found it difficult to nominate the PCF as the party with the most ambivalent attitude towards the idea of Eurocommunism. In

---

[11] See discussion in D. Hine, 'Socialists and Communists in Italy—Reversing Roles?', *West European Politics,* Vol. 1, No. 2, May 1978.

this case, the party's history, leadership, self-image and internal composition have been seen as contributing towards a less easily adaptable posture, both domestically and internationally.[12] Moreover, electoral reactions and the responses of the PCF's political competitors have continued to reflect basic scepticism concerning the willingness and freedom of the party to accommodate itself within the structures and constraints of a pluralist political system. From an oversimplified perspective, the PCF has been far less successful in constructing an appropriate rationale for the changes it has undertaken compared with the PCI or the PCE. Thus the party has been unable to fall back on a reasonably long-established and well-articulated policy of greater independence from the USSR to support its critical gestures between 1975 and 1977. The PCF's attitudes and tactics towards political alliances since 1974 have not been as consistently pursued or as effectively presented as those of the PCI. In addition, the party leadership's concern to shorten the path to power and to exercise influence in the immediate future in a Left coalition government, has given rise to doubts within the party, particularly among those intellectuals and long standing party members who distrust the Socialists and fear a dilution of their own party's goals.

These points appear to underline the marginal role of the PCF in relation to the pressures and responses which have characterised the evolution of the PCI and PCE. It is nevertheless true that, from the particular perspective of the PCF, the modifications in attitudes and policies, and changes of emphasis have not only led to some noticeable rebuffs and altercations in relations with the USSR but also to signs of disorientation and speculation within the party itself. The sudden and rather selective shifts in the alliance tactics within the Union of the Left and in the party's posture *vis-à-vis* the international Communist movement are not as easily explained or, perhaps, dismissed as some interpretations suggest.

The PCF's pursuit of socialism 'in French colours' is more readily traced to its domestic political strategy than reflected or further explored in its involvement with the USSR and in its views on the nature of the international Communist movement. Until the middle of the 1960s the party, under Thorez, could be relied upon to defend wholeheartedly the essential unity of the Communist movement, expressed in the respect due to USSR as the first socialist state, against Togliatti's arguments in favour of polycentrism. The extreme caution with which the party handled the issues arising from de-Stalinisation, indicated not only the PCF's instinctive loyalty to the USSR, but also its belief in the cohesion of the international movement as the vital factor in the ultimate success and expansion of Communism. This basic reflex was

---

[12] For comprehensive discussions of the PCF forming a background to the more recent development see R. Tierski, *French Communism 1920-1974,* Columbia UP, 1974 and A. Kriegel, *The French Communists,* University of Chicago Press, London, 1972. On more recent developments see A. Laurens and T. Pfister, *Les Nouveaux Communistes Aux Portes du Pouvoir,* Stock, Paris, 1977; A. Stiefbold, *The French Communist Party in Transition,* Praeger Special Studies, 1977.

more profoundly disturbed, though still far from being deadened, by the Soviet invasion of Czechoslovakia. The party's immediate and subsequent reactions to the invasion revealed something of its dilemma in relation to the USSR, and its uncertainty over both the domestic and international implications of entering into any open criticism. The Central Committee of the party condemned the invasion (at the cost of resignations and counter attacks) but did not pursue the criticism during the 'normalisation' process until 1972 when the party returned to a defence of its position in response to the trials of Czech dissidents.[13]

It is significant that the PCF's willingness to be more clearly identified as an opponent of the method and rationale behind the USSR's handling of the Czechoslovakian issue surfaced during the period of a major step forward in its domestic strategy, involving negotiations with the Socialist party for a common policy programme of the Left. What is striking about the rhythm of the PCF's relations with the USSR, from 1974 onwards, is the increasing willingness of the leadership, under Marchais, to assert the party's right to determine its own domestic tactics (and reshape a part of its image accordingly) and to be prepared to make its point bluntly. For a brief period between 1974 and the middle of 1975, the PCF and the Soviet Union appeared to move closer together in their approval and encouragement of the Portuguese Communist party's attempt to gain power at the expense of the Portuguese Socialists and tolerance of democratic processes. From the summer of 1975, however, particularly after the Soviet Union's reaffirmation of the dangers of pursuing electoral alliances, the PCF became an almost aggressive exponent of its autonomy in adjusting its strategy to the conditions prevailing in French politics. In a sustained effort to develop the democratic face of French Communism and, as a demonstration of the priority which the PCF gave to justifying its position, the party stepped up its public criticism of the restrictions on cultural and intellectual freedom in the USSR and, more significantly in international terms, moved closer to the views of the PCI and PCE in the preparatory sessions preceding the Berlin Conference. The approach and emphasis of the PCF's Twenty-second Party Congress in February, 1976 and Marchais' independent stance at the Berlin Conference in June of that year, suggested that the party was losing some of its inhibitions in underlining its differences with the USSR.

Those differences are, nevertheless, still confined to a limited area. The continuing reluctance of the party as a whole (as distinct from some individual critics) to go beyond the assertion of the right to determine its domestic priorities, together with the PCF's more general view of its external links, continue to distinguish the party's position from those of the PCI and PCE. While the PCF may have been prepared to recommend the removal of the phrase 'the dictatorship of the proletariat' from the party statutes at its 1976 Congress it did not fully support the substitution of 'international solidarity'

---

13 R. Tierski, *op. cit.*, p. 291-2.

for 'proletarian internationalism' in the final document of the Berlin Conference, seeing in this further signs of a diminished Soviet inspiration for the long term objectives of Communist parties.

It is interesting, though perhaps less significant, to note that something of the PCF's lack of confidence in handling relations with the Soviet Union is reflected in Marchais' rather self-conscious gestures of refusal to attend the CPSU's Twenty-fifth Congress in 1976 and the celebrations marking the Fiftieth anniversary of the October Revolution in November, 1977. Although the PCF was represented on both occasions, Marchais' snub somehow seemed less convincing than Berlinguer's insistence on appearing himself to press home his party's conviction in adhering to its independent line.

If the PCF's domestic strategy, primed for substantial electoral victory at the next election, was the major factor in determining the party's relations with the USSR from 1974 onwards, then the nature and fate of this strategy clearly have a bearing on any evaluation of the party's ability to sustain its changed position into the future. Many of the doubts about the 'sincerity' and effectiveness of the shifts in attitude and approach made by the PCF have been linked to its behaviour in domestic politics; in fact, precisely in the area where the party has insisted on its freedom from outside interference in the exploiting of political alliances with other 'progressive forces'. The party's objective in the 1970s has been to lead a combined Left opposition to a parliamentary victory against the Gaullist and Centre Right groups, while deferring to a future occasion the question of its precise role in a Left coalition over the longer term. Compared with the PCI, the PCF's experience appears neither to have brought it substantially nearer government nor to have resolved the problems of the party's identity and priorities. The major variables from the point of view of the PCF were the strength and militancy of the French Socialist party as its leading partner in the Union of the Left; and these altered between 1973 and 1975 to the disadvantage of the Communists.

The achievement of Socialist-Communist agreement in the 1972 Common Programme increased the combined Left's parliamentary strength in the 1973 elections. More significantly, however, the election results and their interpretation by the PCF gave a foretaste of the rivalry between the party and a rejuvenated Socialist party over the expansion of their electorate and, therefore, their relative influence within the alliance. In 1974, the near success of François Mitterrand as the Presidential candidate of the combined Left did not, in fact, reinforce unity so much as to drive the PCF into a year-long unproductive campaign to seek additional counterweights to the Socialists from disaffected Gaullists and other groups. The PCF's need for, and yet lurking fear of, the Socialists to fulfil at least the first stage in its 'parliamentary road to socialism' produced a combination of concessions and provocations in policy commitments and political tactics in the protracted run-up to the 1978 elections. The final breakdown in the negotiations for the updating of the Common Programme in September, 1977, prevented the Union of the Left strategy from being effectively tested, in the form originally envisaged by the PCF, in the March election. While the PCF managed to maintain (though not expand) its share of the vote in spite of the changes in policy and attitudes towards the Soviet Union, the Left's failure to win the election leaves the PCF with a partially modified image but lacking any immediate incentive or encouragement to continue with its strategy.

A surprisingly vocal and public election post-mortem from opposing standpoints, like Elleinstein and Althusser,[14] has pushed the leadership into deflecting doubts about the soundness and acceptability of its overall political analysis by attacking the Socialist Party's lack of cooperation and commitment to genuine socialist objectives.[15] The internal party debate, itself, indicates something of the PCF's temporary disorientation. To date, the polemics surrounding the advance and retreat of the PCF in grasping the nettle of its role and purpose in both the short and long term have aired frustration rather than provided clearly acceptable answers.

Despite the PCF's constant affirmation since 1976 of a 'socialism in French colours', a number of observers have tried to link the party's increasing aggressiveness in the summer of 1977 to the influence of the Soviet Union. It is difficult to show conclusively that there is such a link. Although the party has throughout this period carefully circumscribed the limits of its disputes with the USSR, its internal interests appear to have been reasonably well served by the bid to gain greater national credibility. That bid has also, however, forced to the surface the issue of the PCF's continued self-image as the 'vanguard of the working class'. The reason for the PCF's precipitation of a break with the Socialist party lies in the unwillingness and unpreparedness of the Communist party, at this stage in its evolution, to face up to the choices brought ever closer by the contemplation of a transitional phase to socialism.

The Partido Comunista de España (PCE)

There are a number of obvious and striking differences which distinguish the PCE from the Italian and French parties both in its relations with the USSR and in the circumstances determining its domestic political strategy. The PCE appears to have suffered from fewer of the inhibitions shown by the PCI and PCF in seeking to balance or limit criticisms of Soviet influence in the international Communist movement. It also seems to have pushed the party's accommodation with the symbolism and procedures of parliamentary democracy, and the gradual pace of political and economic change associated with democratic socialism, further than either the PCI or the PCF. In addition, as a result of the publication of Santiago Carrillo's book *Eurocommunism and the State*, the PCE is sometimes identified (however inappropriately) with a

---

14 Jean Ellenstein, a leading party intellectual and historian who has openly criticised the Soviet Union, and Louis Althusser, a party intellectual sceptical of the PCF's Eurocommunist line.

15 See F. L. Wilson, 'The French CP's Dilemma', *Problems of Communism*, July-August 1978, pp. 7-12.

doctrinal text, providing a theoretical justification for the tactics and objectives of 'Eurocommunist' parties.[16]

At the same time, compared with the electoral strength and parliamentary representation of the PCI and PCF (or even with the latter's votes in the immediate post-war years) the PCE is, as yet, in a much weaker position in domestic politics. Within the international Communist movement the party's influence and significance was conditioned until 1977 by its exile from the Spanish political arena. It has tended to identify with the PCI's articulation of the 'autonomous' approach rather than to develop a particularly distinct rationale of its own. It is nevertheless true that the PCE has frequently been at the centre of discussions and controversies concerning the changes in West European communism, for the major reason that the leadership's critique of the political context of socialism in the USSR has presented the most overt challenge to the stature of the Soviet Union and its links with other ruling and non-ruling parties.

The distance which the PCE has travelled from its close identification with, if not dependence on, the USSR during and after the civil war, to its publicly bitter debate with the Soviet leadership and press in 1977, illustrates the extent to which the party's expectations and assumptions about its political role and priorities have changed.

After 1956, the exiled PCE's pro-Soviet focus began to waver under the pressures of the party's repudiation of its earlier Stalinist sympathies and the search for a more realistic strategy to make some impact against the Franco regime. Carrillo's increasing influence after 1960 and his determination to move the party towards a policy of 'national reconciliation' with anti-Fascist forces further enhanced the party's independent inclinations. The major turning point, prefiguring the ideological disputes and public hostility of the 1975-77 period, came in 1968. The PCE's internal structure, political assumptions and international orientation were all fundamentally shaken by the Soviet invasion of Czechoslovakia. Allegedly the party came close to a complete break with the USSR in condemning the invasion, at the cost of provoking a split in the leadership which finally led in 1969 to the resignation of Garcia, the Secretary for Organisation, and the expulsion of Gomez another member of the Central Committee.[17] The USSR's withdrawal of funds from the PCE and its active assistance to the emergence of a pro-Moscow faction, though ultimately unsuccessful, thereafter reinforced the caution of the leadership and provided further incentive for the PCE's development of closer relations with the PCI and the Roumanian and Yugoslav parties.

A major factor in the subsequent relationship between the USSR and the PCE has been the PCE's increasing preoccupation with the competition for influence and manoeuvre in Spanish politics preceding and following the end

---

[16] See for example Eric Heffer's review of *Eurocommunism and the State* in *Labour Weekly,* 16 December, 1977.

[17] On this point see discussion in G. Hermet, *The Communists in Spain,* Saxon House Lexington, 1974, pp. 77-82.

of the Franco regime. Two features of this relationship have been particularly noticeable. Firstly, in the international context Carrillo has been at pains to give the PCE the appearance of greater independence, by emphasising the differences between the party and the CPSU and also by linking the PCE's position to a more pronounced West European orientation. Secondly, the party leadership has attempted to raise some of the issues connected with a potentially protracted transitional period to socialism (especially in the Spanish context) and the reconciliation of socialism with democratic liberties. Carrillo's prominent stand before and during the Berlin Conference of Communist parties in 1976 and his refusal to attend the Twenty-fifth Congress of the CPSU, preferring to meet with Italian political leaders in Rome, were two well-publicised manifestations of the PCE leader's lack of concern for muting the effects of his challenge. The PCE was not alone in insisting on the need to adjust the orthodox Soviet models of a socialist state to the requirements of the pluralist traditions of Western Europe. Nevertheless, the Soviet attack against Carrillo's (again uninhibited) book, published immediately following the Spanish election in June 1977, was designed to isolate the PCE and underline its marginal importance. In fact, Carrillo turned the debate to the party's own advantage in laying further claim to promoting a democratic alternative in the jostling for position and influence with the Partido Socialista Obrero Español (PSOE) which was renewed in the months after the election.

The PCE in developing a domestic strategy made increasingly urgent by the signs of the weakening in the Franco regime from 1974 onwards showed, like the PCI in Italian politics, an awareness of the need to establish the party's credentials as a legitimate participant in the political process. In the case of the PCE, however, this lack of legitimisation was far more basic given the long exile of the party and its fear of the survival of civil war memories, particularly among the party's prospective supporters on the Left. The PCE's immediate and central purpose in the period following the death of Franco was to translate its organisational advantage compared with other parties into public acceptability, while maximising support for a rapid and complete break with the Francoist political framework.[18] The ability of King Juan Carlos and his prime minister Suarez, to prolong and to manage effectively the post-Franco transition period, ended any lingering hopes of the PCE of organising a coalition to seize the initiative in creating a provisional government. The focus of the party's activities, both internally and externally, turned on securing support for its full legalisation as an essential part of the moves towards political reform, particularly since the government appeared to exercise tolerance towards its frequently more militant competitor, the PSOE. Following the PCE's legalisation, its ensuing electoral campaign in June 1977 and subsequent reflections on its share of the vote (9.2 per cent compared with

---

[18] For an exploration of the domestic tactics of the PCE see Eusebio Mujal-Leon, 'The PCE in Spanish Politics', *Problems of Communism,* July-August, 1978.

30

the PSOE's 29.3 per cent) indicated its continuing concern to allay fears about its commitment to the newly established democratic procedures. This led, on the one hand, to a readiness, particularly on the part of the leadership, to emphasise its responsible image by supporting (more enthusiastically than the PSOE) the government's offer of a limited political and economic 'truce' in the Moncloa Pact of October, 1977.[19] On the other, the PCE's internal evolution reached the point at its Ninth Congress in April, 1978, of agreeing, though not without lively debate and continuing reservations, to drop Leninism from the party statutes.[20] The PCE's determination to continue the strategy of winning credibility as a 'responsible' party in the election in 1979 following the endorsement of Spain's new democratic constitution, achieved for the party a disappointingly meagre one per cent improvement in its share of the vote.

While the PCE's evolution in the 1970s is explicable in terms of its view of the need to prepare for the transition from dictatorship to democracy, the party's perceptions of its future must remain uncertain or at least confined to determining its place in the opposition. Carrillo's control over the party and its intense concentration on re-establishing its political base in Spain have so far contained any real conflicts which might be anticipated from the steps the party has taken to reshape its internal and international stance. The likelihood of conflicts emerging, as well as the benefits to be gained from any further substantial concessions, are difficult to envisage in the short term.

The major question mark seems to be whether the ability of the PCE to make significant inroads into the PSOE electorate will depend on its conceding more in its policies, party structure and commitment to a fundamental transformation of society. As a number of observers have noted, such concessions not only threaten to weaken the PCE's bargaining position with the PSOE but bring the party closer than either the PCI or PCF to the threshold of an identity crisis.

Foreign Policy and Domestic Politics
This rather summary exploration of some of the major features of the circumstances and impulses shaping the attitudes of the three Communist parties towards their respective priorities, has demonstrated the usefulness of uncovering national and individual party differences. Clearly, these differences will influence the ability of, and necessity for the parties to maintain or extend their strategies into the future; they also underline variations in the content and emphasis of their current stances on international issues. The impact of their domestic political preoccupations on foreign policy is especially interesting.

---

[19] The Moncloa Pact was an agreement on economic and political objectives signed by all the major parties in Spain in October, 1977 and cited by the PCE as evidence of its commitment to a 'responsible' programme.

[20] *Ibid.*, pp. 33-35.

The relationship between domestic legitimacy, political effectiveness and a less threatening external posture has not been seen in entirely the same light in Italy, Spain and France. On the one hand, the PCI and PCE have viewed the relationship as demanding some recognition of a national interest 'core' in foreign policy to create a bridge between themselves and other major political groups beyond those of the Left. On the other hand in France, the PCF has largely interpreted the relationship as one requiring some rapprochement between its views and those of its competitors on the Left on the link envisaged between domestic transformation and broader international objectives. The militant and anti-capitalist orientation of the French Socialist party between 1972 and 1978 sharpened the party's image and narrowed the gap between the Socialists' plans for radical domestic socio-economic reform and the previous conciliatory posture in international and especially European affairs. The PCF has, therefore, been under somewhat less pressure from that particular source to alter its own approach drastically in the interests of maximising the unity and appeal of a coalition of the Left.

It is worth distinguishing between two separate factors which appear to have influenced the Communist parties' calculations concerning their foreign policies. The first, an awareness of the link between domestic choices and international constraints, is less easy to pinpoint clearly than the second, the impact of foreign policy issues on party policies and their perceived relevance to electoral competition. Uncertainty and caution over the first of these factors seems justified, given the room for declaratory and ritual acknowledgement of international constraints (by all parties) which makes the problem of determining their precise impact all the more difficult. One of the most fundamental aspects of the West European Communist parties' interpretation of the post-war international framework has been their insistence that the structure of relationships associated with the cold war and the central role of the United States in Western Europe have provided the channels for the exploitation of the proletariat and the sharpening of class conflict. This was held to be true, not only because the allegedly capitalist and imperialist, US-orchestrated network of economic and military ties did not serve the working class, but also because it undermined national independence in Western Europe. An analysis of this kind left no option but to foresee a complete break with American or capitalist-inspired Atlantic and West European links in the event of a transition to socialist regimes and policies. Yet by the mid 1970s both the PCI and PCE were indicating their acknowledgement of a range of external economic constraints, closely bound up with the nature of the international capitalist economy which, at the very least, would affect the direction of their economic and industrial programmes. In the case of the PCI, as we shall see in a subsequent chapter, the specific questions involved in, and the extent of Italian dependence upon, the European Community crystallised the issue of the balance of threats and advantages involved in coming to terms with the intensification of international economic activity since the 1950s.

The extent to which the domestic context and domestic preoccupations have had an effect on reducing the Communist parties' intransigence towards the international environment has differed, as between Italy and Spain on the one hand, and France on the other. In Italy a perception of the interrelationship between the country's political régime, internal stability and its participation in the Western Alliance and European institutions has been particularly acute and widely noted.[21] It was strongly articulated by the Christian Democrats in the interests of their own survival after the war and taken up by the Socialists in a demonstration of their credentials as a governing party in the 1960s. The PCI's partial softening of its previous total rejection of such a relationship (or one-way leverage as the party preferred to see it) has been the result of a change in its assessment of Italy's economic and political vulnerability. This has led to the position, developed by Berlinguer and several party spokesmen between 1973 and 1976, of the party condoning Italy's involvement in the Western international framework, partly from a recognition of the irreversible features of Italian post-war economic development, and partly from a conviction that it would be too dangerous for the survival of a radical government to provoke a sharp break. (It would also be an unacceptable demand for a party anxious to enter into an 'historic compromise' with the Christian Democrats.) At the same time, the PCI has indicated that it sees such involvement as manageable in the sense of it being possible to reduce some of the undesirable features of the external constraints. Thus, in the case of the European Community and NATO, accommodation is tempered by the PCI's advocacy of institutional and policy reform of the former and a minimal commitment of Italy to the latter. Hence, it is arguable that the PCI's attitude to international links is not that they provide a positive support for the domestic status quo but that they represent a necessity. The party must continue to accept these links in order to discourage either internal or external forces from finding grounds for challenging the PCI's acceptability as a party of government in the eyes of the rest of the international community.

In Spain the awareness of external constraints on domestic choices has been partly conditioned by the sense of relative isolation induced by the Franco regime's restricted involvement in the framework of West European relations. However, if the perception of any extensive political or military constraint has been absent, the extent to which the Spanish economy has become dependent on a range of international economic relationships has affected assessments of both internal economic and political choices. The PCE has responded most visibly to the consequences of Spain's links with the international economy by, in a way, advocating the extension and formalisation of some external constraints in its enthusiastic support of Spain's membership of the European Community. In more declaratory terms, which make it difficult to determine the party's actual perceptions of external constraints on future domestic

---

[21] For a full discussion of this point see P. Vannicelli, *Italy, NATO and the European Community,* Harvard Studies in International Affairs, No. 31, Harvard University, 1974.

options, the PCE has emphasised the importance of the West European dimension to Spain's political development towards democracy.

By contrast, the domestic context in France and the political debate on the Left have failed to produce conditions to make it either necessary or prudent for the PCF to modify substantially its attitude of confrontation with a hostile international environment.[22] The Gaullist tradition of asserting (albeit often symbolically) French resistance to external constraints, where these implied French subordination or insensitive treatment, provided a quite different setting compared with the assumptions built up by the Christian Democrats in Italy. The PCF has, in this sense, found itself in conformity with national preoccupations, though for quite different reasons from those inspiring the Gaullists. In addition, the PCF's main target in its domestic strategy, the Socialist party, has moved further in the direction of the PCF under the influence of the more confrontational attitude of the CERES[23] group towards the impact of external influences on the French economy. Finally, while the PCF has voiced its fears for the fate of a socialist government in France in the future, given its need to survive in a more than suspicious international climate, its conclusions in 1977 suggest an underlying consistency in its position. In a revealing contrast with the cautious approach of the PCI, Marchais' anticipation of the vulnerability of a future Left government led him not to advise the party to find some way of appeasing suspicions in advance, but to justifying the retention of the 'force de frappe' partly as a means of deterring threats to the integrity of the socialist state.[24]

The second factor which has influenced the parties' foreign policy calculations concerns the importance of foreign policy issues in domestic political competition. As we have seen, the degree of recognition of external constraints on domestic choices in all three countries has not been unrelated to the party battle, and the anticipation of future decisions and policies which would have to be made inside coalitions of greater or less cohesion. The extent to which the Communist parties have been prepared to raise foreign policy issues in the pursuit of domestic strategies for increasing electoral support and access to government influence has depended on two factors; the potential of such issues for enhancing the parties' national legitimacy and their relevance and negotiability in the construction of political alliances.

There is clearly a close connection between these two factors, expressed most visibly in Italy. The Christian Democratic party's own sense of legitimacy and national identification has relied heavily on stressing particular themes in foreign policy which have defined the terms of the debate with the PCI. The connection is less directly expressed in both Spain and France. In Spain, the

---

[22] See M. Harrison, 'A Socialist Foreign Policy for France', *ORBIS,* 4, Winter 1976.

[23] The initials stand for Centre d'Études de Recherches et d'Éducation Socialiste. It is the leading left wing faction within the French Socialist party and is represented in the Party's Secretariat.

[24] *Le Monde,* 5 August, 1978.

PCE's interest in building up a broad coalition of anti-Fascist forces in advance of Franco's departure brought it into contact with parties whose attitudes towards Spain's future external orientation, with the exception of membership of the EEC, were not very emphatic. In France, the Socialist's party's own internal divisions and uncertainty over France's external posture (*viz.* its partial critique of both the Gaullist position on the European Community and Giscard d'Estaing's 'neo-Atlanticism') have provided neither a clear alternative nor a total endorsement of the prevailing conception of national interests with which the PCF might be expected to associate itself. Instead, of course, the PCF has taken its cue concerning identification with national symbols from the Gaullists.

The need to make use of foreign policy issues to achieve national (as distinct from merely democratic) legitimacy has been seen in different ways and given greater or less importance by the three parties. In one sense, of course, the 'legitimising' task of the Communist parties starts, and conceivably ends, with the Soviet relationship. In foreign policy, 'transmission belt' fears, raised by the USSR's past use of West European Communist parties as internal advocates of its foreign policy goals, have been widely expressed in relation to their reliability in organisations such as NATO. Yet a complete reversal of relationships is out of the question for the cohesion, even existence of the parties themselves. It is, therefore, more the case of parties recognising that some issues may have a more significant impact on their legitimacy than others.

Arguably, the PCE has tended to look inwards to the national flag and monarchy for symbols through which to promote its national legitimacy in the absence of a clear equivalent in Spain's external commitments. Nevertheless, the party's endorsement of Spain's entry into the European Community could be seen as a calculation by the PCE that EC membership will come to be the cornerstone of Spain's future involvement in Western Europe; support for membership will be regarded as an essential element in the platform of any party aspiring to take part in government.

In France, the 'terms' for national legitimacy have, as we noted earlier, been defined differently. They have turned on adherence to the principle of national independence linked to, and in some respects derived from, anti-Americanism tempered by a recognition that the basic security tie with the Atlantic Alliance cannot yet be totally abrogated. The first two of these have presented the PCF with little difficulty, the party finding no incompatibility with its own analysis of French needs.[25] Competition with the Gaullists to upbid one another in promoting national assertiveness has been seen as the refuge of the PCF in its striking out away from the Soviet Union. The third element has also been recognised by the party to the extent that it has modified its outright confrontation, moving away from its ambiguous position in 1972 and

---

[25] See comments made by Jacques Huntzinger on the foreign policy of the PCF, *Le Monde*, 3 October, 1977.

affirming by 1976 France's membership of the Atlantic Treaty until such time as the two blocs are dissolved. However, the party has not sought to emphasise this minimal commitment nor to rely on it for furthering its national profile.

A more dramatic statement of what clearly could be interpreted as a bid for greater national acceptance was the PCF's decision in May, 1977 to reverse its total opposition to the 'force de frappe' and to support the maintenance of the nuclear weapon as a necessary part of France's national defence. More will be said in Chapter IV concerning the reservations and ambiguities of the party's position on this issue which make it improbable that the PCF could claim the benefit which might otherwise be expected to flow from identification with such a symbol of French national and military priorities. However, it is worth noting that the move interrupted the Socialist party's own internal discussions on its attitude towards the 'force de frappe' and allowed the PCF to challenge its indecisiveness and particularly Mitterrand's suggestion that the issue of the nuclear weapon should be put to a referendum. Jean Kanapa, until his death in September 1978, the PCF's foreign policy spokesman, pointedly remarked that nothing could take away the responsibility of government for France's national defence, and that the PCF felt it had an obligation to spell out in the Common Programme a clear and effective defence policy.[26]

The two most important influences which have contributed to the PCI's awareness of the link between foreign policy and national legitimacy have been the impact on domestic politics of the polarisation of attitudes towards Italy's external links and the party's commitment to pursuing the 'historic compromise' strategy with the Christian Democrats. The PCI rejected the assumptions and mechanisms behind the post-war Western Alliance. This, combined with the party's Soviet links, exposed it to suspicion and, after the Socialist party's reappraisal of its own attitudes in the early 1960's, to isolation. The success with which the Christian Democrats built up a framework of values and expectations, associated with the promotion of Italian internal and external interests via its international alignment effectively challenged the PCI to disavow these interests and risk further exclusion from political influence. The PCI began to soften its position on the European Community without the immediate incentive of the prospect of a historic compromise strategy on the horizon. However, it has been the latter which has appeared to cause the PCI to re-examine its approach on foreign policy. In particular, the party leadership chose to focus attention between 1975 and 1976 on the PCI's acknowledgement of the undesirability of withdrawing Italy from NATO, using the issue to demonstrate the PCI's readiness to take a responsible attitude both towards international detente and towards the PCI's potential political partners.

Thus, 'we do not raise the question of Italy's withdrawal from the Atlantic Alliance, since such a move, just as any other withdrawal from one or the other bloc . . . would not only be unrealistic but would in the end have the

---

26 L'Humanité, 27 July, 1977.

effect of hindering or even reversing the process of international detente. . . . If we were to set withdrawal from NATO as an absolute condition, it would, internally mean re-opening a division within the popular and democratic forces of our country; this would weaken rather than broaden and strengthen the mass, united bases of the Italian democratic state, and consequently its real independence and sovereignity.'[27]

The timing and selection of the NATO issue were closely related to the tactics of the Christian Democrats in the run-up to the 1976 election. These were designed to draw attention to the PCI's vulnerability in the defence of Italian external interests in order to shift the debate away from the Christian Democrats' own domestic weaknesses.[28] For the PCI, electoral considerations coincided with the need to allay the fundamental suspicions of members of the Christian Democrat party who used the international issue as grounds for denying the necessity for Communist participation in government. Thus, in Italy the wider question of enhancing national legitimacy has been dominated by the PCI's perceptions of the preoccupations of its anticipated coalition partner. These perceptions were reflected further in the PCI's moves in 1977 to open up the debate on aspects of its relations with the United States and its attempts to create a more direct dialogue through well-publicised visits of PCI leaders.

It follows from what has been said so far that the relevance and negotiability of foreign policy issues in the construction of domestic alliances by the PCI, PCF and PCE have depended on the political character of the alliances, their objectives and, indeed, the extent to which they have been formalised. The PCE's interest in, or ability to promote, an alliance strategy has been part of the process of transition from the Franco régime. It has made use of foreign policy issues, particularly support of the European Community and toleration of the American military bases in Spain, to indicate its general willingness to cooperate with anti-Fascist political forces for initially short-term domestic goals. In this sense, the PCE's approach is comparable with that of the PCI, whose more explicit and narrowly focussed strategy towards the Christian Democrats has persuaded the party to emphasise certain themes in its foreign policy. The ability of the PCI to negotiate the foreign policy agenda has so far been constrained by its prime concern to avoid weakening its bargaining position with the Christian Democrats until either its electoral strength has increased or it is conceded a formal role in government.

By contrast, the more formal and programmatic nature of the PCI's alliance with the Union of the Left, at least until September 1977, created a quite different framework for bargaining over foreign policy issues. The foreign

---

[27] E. Berlinguer, Report to the Fourteenth Congress of the PCI, March 18, 1975, quoted in D. Sassoon, *op. cit.,* pp. 54-55.

[28] For further details on the PCI's approach to foreign policy in the 1976 elections see, R. Putnam, 'Italian Foreign Policy: the Emergent Consensus' in H. R. Penniman (ed.), *Italy at the Polls, The Parliamentary Elections of 1976,* Washington, American Enterprise Institute for Public Policy Research, 1977.

policy section of the 1972 Common Programme had been drafted to paper over major differences between the Socialist party and the PCF, particularly in relation to France's membership of the Atlantic Alliance and role in the European Community. By 1977 when discussions resumed within the Union of the Left to update the Common Programme for the 1978 elections, the positions of both the PCF and the Socialist party had either changed or were undergoing change in such a way as to make the resolution of differences easier on some issues such as the European Community and membership of the Alliance, while re-opening others, such as the 1972 agreement on the abandonment of France's nuclear weapon.

The overwhelming domestic priorities and preoccupation with the 1978 election possibilities of the Union of the Left reinforced the inclination of the parties to play down differences in emphasis and significant conflicts over policy on external issues. However, the unilateral approach of the PCF towards adjusting its foreign policy position from the spring of 1977 onwards, sharpened sensitivities on all sides and underlined the growing competitiveness between the PCF and Parti Socialiste (PS). The PCF Central Committee's decision in May, 1977 to retain the 'force de frappe', justified as an unavoidable accommodation with the prevailing structure of France's national defence resources, sparked off an increasingly bitter debate with the Socialist party, culminating in the effective collapse of the alliance in September, 1977. Two factors contributed to the polemics on both sides. The PCF's apparent sudden reversal of its previous outright opposition raised suspicions in the minds of the Socialists concerning the motives of the PCF, both in relation to its electoral bid and its commitment to the Left alliance itself. This was compounded by the Socialist party's own internal divisions on the fate of the nuclear weapon, evident from the advancing of arguments from members of the party's Defence Commission in favour of rallying the Left behind its retention. The Socialist party's intention of convening a special congress to debate the issue only added to the discomfort of its leadership at being made to respond to the more rapid decision-making processes of the PCF. On the other hand, Marchais' insistence that the issue of France's deterrent capacity could not be blurred in the Common Programme, still less resolved by a national referendum, conceivably owed something to his own concern to cut short debate which was beginning to surface within the PCF.[29] The divisions between the two parties over the financial and military implications of a commitment to retaining the 'force de frappe', even if only in the short term, its targeting, and the decision-making procedures for its use, opened up more fundamental differences over the direction of French foreign policy. Although these were not pursued further in advance of the 1978 election they remain on the future agenda in the event of renewed attempts to develop a joint, alternative foreign

---

[29] *Le Monde*, 6 June 1977 quoted interview with Charles Fizbin, first secretary of the PCF Paris Federation, with France-Nouvelle in which he referred to the intra-party debate on retention of nuclear weapons between the party's younger cadres and the older generation of party militants.

and defence policy for the French Left. Opinions are still divided as to which issue was the vital one in provoking the crisis in the Union of the Left. Differences over the future of the nuclear weapon surfaced together with public disagreements on a number of major domestic issues. It is clear, however, that had the alliance succeeded, the nuclear weapons issue would have been one amongst a range of foreign policy matters which would have posed serious obstacles in the way of a smoothly functioning Socialist-Communist coalition.

Discussion of the differences amongst the PCI, PCF and PCE concerning the nature and extent of their moves towards greater independence of the USSR and changes in their domestic strategies, indicate some recurring themes in the parties' foreign policy tactics and preoccupations. Given a common concern to strengthen their electoral position and their status *vis-à-vis* their major political competitors, their focus has inevitably been selective. Seen from the domestic perspective there is an element of consistency in the PCI and PCE's more accommodating posture in their domestic contexts and their stance in foreign policy. The PCF's more overt confrontational role, as part of the Union of the Left, while it has involved concessions by the PCF towards its domestic political partners, has enabled the party to retain a more aggressive, if less rigid, position on some foreign policy issues. The consequences of this difference for the more detailed aspects of the parties' changes in foreign policy will be explored more fully in the next chapter.

IV The International Context: Opportunities and Constraints

When viewed through a domestic lens, the partial adjustment of foreign policy positions by the PCI, PCF and PCE can be brought into reasonably clear focus. A change of angle, however, reveals a somewhat more cloudy image. In moving from the domestic to the international context, the objectives and rationale supporting the parties' domestic strategies, and thus the foreign policy gestures which have been a spin-off from them, become less well defined.

Much of the discussion of the political impact or the desirability of the Communist parties expanding their electoral support has been conducted in terms of the feasible options for achieving political change at the national level. On the whole, at the international level, the debate has centred not so much on positive consideration of the options for change as the extent of anticipated disruption to the status quo. The attitudes and preoccupations of the major external interests, the USA and USSR, have, in themselves, contributed to the narrowing of horizons. Another factor has been the disjointed nature of the changes made in their foreign policies and international postures by the parties, the result of blending domestic needs with continuing international loyalties and instinctive reflexes. Most observers have pointed to the persistent conformity of the PCI, PCF and PCE with substantial areas and principles of Soviet foreign policy. This has been seen as fundamental and indicative of the inability of the parties to sustain an independent and critical role internationally which would allow them to adapt existing Western-oriented relationships to their own requirements. In other words, while foreign policy adjustments may temporarily strengthen domestic credibility, placed in their international context they appear either tenuous or ultimately too threatening for all sides to be absorbed without provoking confrontation. It is interesting to speculate on the extent to which future coalition governments, involving Communist parties, would identify unhesitatingly with Soviet foreign policy priorities in circumstances where broader government or coalition objectives might set up strong counter pressures; or, alternatively whether the United States, out of conviction, or under domestic pressure, would require precise commitments from governments including the PCI and PCF as a condition for their remaining in the Atlantic Alliance.

Indeed, the extent to which the external reverberations of internal political changes associated with the PCI, PCF and PCE could be contained or channelled, or would trigger a further chain of events within the framework of European relations depends on several factors: the correspondence between the emphasis of the parties on national priorities and the existing, or possibly newly emerging network of common interests represented in the Atlantic or Western European framework; their ability to develop and implement an independent and radical foreign policy and their perception of the importance and timing of foreign policy changes for supporting domestic, political and economic transformation.

In this light it is tempting to pose a question which contrasts with the focus in the previous chapter on foreign policy in domestic politics. Do the limited foreign policy moves of the PCI, PCF and PCE suggest in any way that they have begun to consider the substantive issues involved in relating foreign policy to the strategy for 'national roads to socialism', and the demands created by the prospect of a possibly extended, transitional phase? One possible short and dismissive answer might be that the evaluation of detente, the slight adjustment of pro-Soviet and anti-American sentiment and tolerance of NATO and the EC are merely palliatives at the international level. They present no serious challenge to the view of the world divided into imperialist and anti-imperialist forces which provides the parties with their basic criterion for measuring commitment or opposition in foreign policy, irrespective of national needs. Such has been the view of a number of the PCI's detractors both within and outside Italy. On the other hand, competing pressures may also be at work. It is arguable that circumstances of more sustained electoral competition, and the priority given to safeguarding radical governments against possible charges of threatening the international status quo raise the costs of defaulting on the foreign policy concessions already made.

Before turning to a fuller discussion of these concessions it will be useful to bear in mind some of the main areas of change, reassessment and choice in the foreign policy frameworks of Western Europe in general and of France, Italy and Spain in particular, in the light of which the attitudes and objectives of the PCI, PCF and PCE can, to some extent, be considered. This brief outline might serve as a kind of international equivalent to the changes in domestic political conditions and pressures which have created the context for the parties' formulation of their national strategies.

At the level of Western Europe as a whole there are three principal areas which provide the agenda for choices and strategies in foreign policy. These are, firstly, the familiar territory of European-American relations both within and beyond the confines of NATO and the Atlantic Alliance; secondly, the prospect of a more organised and cohesive foreign policy grouping centred on the political cooperation machinery of the European Community; thirdly, the rather more indeterminate, and wider multilateral framework brought into being by the Conference on Security and Co-operation in Europe which may have a bearing on the handling of certain kinds of issues in East-West European relations. Far from being mutually exclusive, these multilateral arenas reflect an extensive overlap of interests and political relationships.

They also raise questions of future commitments which will depend, in part, on the different priorities of individual governments. From the point of view of West European states, questions of choice and strategy are likely to turn partly on the reconciliation of national aims with collective goals and priorities, and partly on the ability to adopt existing relationships to accommodate new pressures and increased competition of interests between Western Europe and the United States. When these choices are linked to the apparently much more tentative moves of the PCI, PCF and PCE in the direction of limited tolerance of the Atlantic and Community frameworks, it can be seen that their foreign policy challenges and concessions have not been made against a backdrop of absolute consensus.

At the risk of grossly distorting and oversimplifying the complex arena of European-American relations, it may be said that a significant feature of the phases through which the various bilateral and multilateral relationships have passed in the 1970s has been the eruption of substantial political and economic differences between Western Europe and the United States. There have also been overt expressions of dependence by countries like Germany, Italy and the UK on the diplomacy of the United States demonstrated, for example, in the aftermath of the 1973 oil crisis. These have generated continuing uncertainty and resentment within Western Europe over sensitive questions such as the balancing of interests and the sometimes rather aggressive diplomatic tactics employed by the United States in the attempt to get Western Europe to overcome its national divisions.[1] This is very far from saying that friction between Western Europe and the United States has reached the stage where the critique advanced by the PCF and the PCI finds a totally sympathetic response from other political parties. Major differences in the interpretation of the whole security dimension of the Atlantic Alliance prevent any close alignment of views. Nevertheless, it might be suggested that the Communist parties' evaluation of the nature of American involvement in Western Europe is not totally divorced from the misgivings of some governments and their preoccupations regarding their future needs and strategies. In a specific reference which helps make the general point Stanley Hoffman has noted, 'there are many non-communists who believe that either domestic national priorities or West European priorities, which require planning, should be given precedence over the maintenance of the 'open' capitalist Atlantic economy; indeed, that they entail the regulation of foreign investments, or the control of

---

[1] For a fuller discussion of European-American relations see M. Smith, 'From the 'Year of Europe' to a Year of Carter: Continuing Patterns and Problems in Euro-American Relations', *Journal of Common Market Studies,* Vol. XVII, 1978.

capital movements, or the building of a separate money bloc.'[2] There is clearly a major difference between the voicing of such views by a variety of political and economic groups and their being given serious consideration by governments. At the same time, evidence of increasing frustration at the lack of appropriate responses on monetary and trade issues (as seen from the Western European side) have undermined confidence in the ease and manner with which American and Western European interests could be reconciled.

The option in relation to the European Community's foreign policy co-operation is less one of adapting an increasingly strained network to future foreign policy needs, than of investing commitment in, and acknowledging the representativeness of, a framework for asserting specifically West European interests. The ability of the political co-operation machinery of the European Community to fulfil such a role has still to be fully determined. It has so far not succeeded in making an impact in a substantive sense on foreign policy issues which would confirm its status or appeal in relation to the priorities of the most significant of the member states. However, there are a number of distinct areas, or evolving relationships, where the political and economic centrality of the Community framework corresponds with a range of interests of all the participants involved. Here a foreign policy dimension may well become increasingly visible and more demanding in the development of common positions. Examples include the politico-economic aspects of change and stability in the Mediterranean area and the implications of further progress in the Euro-Arab dialogue.[3] To the extent that the political co-operation machinery requires the observance of collective procedures and provides incentives for the convergence of particular demands or special interests, it could conceivably be exploited for the purposes of asserting greater regional independence. This remains largely conjectural in the absence of any real determination to turn national reservations and dissatisfaction,[4] into a solid regional alternative. The motives and continuing divisions revealed in the attempt to use the political co-operation network to develop a common and distinctive policy on the Middle East illustrate both the potential and the obstacles involved. The capacity of the Community's political co-operation procedure to absorb either a challenge to the assumptions behind attempts to seek a foreign policy consensus, or simply indifference to its existence (both being possible responses of future radically inclined governments) is thus difficult to assess. If it is assumed at this point that outright confrontation is both unlikely and, given the fragmentation of interests hitherto, unnecessary, it could well be that the accommodation of governments with Communist party representation, within the political co-operation framework, will depend

2 S. Hoffmann, 'Uneven Allies: An Overview' in D. S. Landes (ed.), *Western Europe: The Trials of Partnership,* Lexington, DC Heath, 1977, p. 79.

3 For a discussion of Western European interests in the Euro-Arab dialogue see D. Allen, 'The Euro-Arab Dialogue', *Journal of Common Market Studies,* Vol. XVII, 1978.

4 For example, concern over the tendency of some Middle Eastern states to identify West European positions automatically with American objectives.

as much on the attitudes and expectations of other participants as it will on the sensitivities of the Communist parties themselves.

Changing East-West relations in Europe represent a third area where foreign policy choices and strategies are likely to be affected by a re-shaping of the framework and, in this case, a more explicit definition of the agenda for the development of future relationships. In some ways the 'CSCE process',[5] partly formalised in a set of principles, partly a matter of good faith and reciprocal response in the absence of permanent institutions, is more difficult to visualise in terms of the consensus or conflicts of interest which will determine the West European approach. In two of the major areas where changes are anticipated by the Helsinki Final Act, namely, a reduction in the tension associated with the presence of two military blocs and further development of trade and economic links, the priorities and pace of changes are likely to be subject to the preoccupations and procedures of NATO and the European Community. The emphasis accorded to issues of human rights and the greater freedom of movement and contact between East and West Europe, will be a matter for choice and judgement in both bilateral and multilateral relations. The overlap of issues and institutional links thus makes the East-West European dimension less clearly separable from the Atlantic and the Community networks. The significance and contribution of the 'CSCE process' for West European foreign policy lie primarily with the moulding of perceptions and expectations of future behaviour. To this could be added the new opportunity to focus specifically on problems of intra-European relations, in a more genuinely multilateral context than that associated with the dialogue dominated by the mutual concerns of the USA and USSR and their alliance systems. In both cases, possibilities exist at the national level within Western Europe for differences of opinion over principles and tactics in the justification and implementation of moves to relax barriers still further. In this context, PCF and PCI participation in government could sharpen sensitivities considerably. Their much less critical interpretation of the motives and behaviour of East European states, particularly the USSR, and their emphasis on the importance of intra-European relations at the expense of bloc priorities and constraints, would create additional hazards for other West European governments in calculating the advantages of maintaining a common front.

The three dimensions of the foreign policy environment in Western Europe outlined, clearly do not exhaust the sources and potential for consensus, dissension and change. Nor do they in any way span the whole range of issues which surface, or are likely to surface, in Europe and in the foreign policies of individual states. For the purposes of this discussion they can be seen as the basic, multilateral frameworks within which, to a greater or less extent, depending on the issue and government in question, regional attitudes and responses are determined. The conflicts of interest, hesitancy and uncertainty

---

[5] Conference for Security and Co-operation in Europe, an international conference leading to the signing of the Helsinki Final Act in August, 1975.

already reflected in the Atlantic, Community and East-West European frameworks are worth bearing in mind in the face of the tendency to measure the foreign policy changes of the PCI, PCF and PCE against the often rather optimistic estimate of Atlantic or West European solidarity.

There are obvious differences in the positions and attitudes of Italy, France and Spain, particularly *vis-à-vis* the Atlantic and Community dimensions, which affect the climate for foreign policy strategies and the likelihood and pattern of any prospective changes. The relevance and influence of both the Atlantic and Community frameworks are most visible in respect of Italy, least, as yet, for Spain, while France continues to maintain its distance from the former. Leaving aside, for a moment, the potential impact of the PCI, PCF and PCE on foreign policy, a brief comment on each of the national contexts may help to suggest the terms within which the possibility of change or future choices can be considered. These can be summarised as follows, beginning at one end of the spectrum with France, moving via Italy to Spain at the other: the attenuation and/or redirection of a previously highly active and independent foreign policy; the activation of a foreign policy previously characterised by passivity and dependence; and the opportunity for a clear commitment to a foreign policy where previously domestic conditions and international reactions had made this inappropriate.

Firstly, in France, the effects of Giscard d'Estaing's Presidency have been to soften confrontation with the USA at least in some areas, and to fulfil the Gaullist predisposition for independent initiatives by adopting, in international economic diplomacy, a role of broker between the industrialised and the less-developed world, which obliquely draws attention to the political incapacity or, indeed, the threatened hegemony of the two super powers. In 'Giscardian' terms, the recognition of 'global interdependence' is accorded greater emphasis than absolute adherence to defence of national interests and independence. (There has been, of course, more than an element of pure symbolism in both.) In addition, the need to focus on French domestic economic difficulties has been seen by some as a factor diverting Presidential attention and resources away from commitment to a highly active foreign policy.[6] So far, however, these partial adjustments in tone and emphasis have not led to any moves sufficient to provoke a re-examination of the overall objectives and assumptions of French foreign policy. Hence, in the absence of a major shift in the political complexion of government, the boundaries of the foreign policy debate are set by the changes, on the whole at the margin, which may result from Giscard d'Estaing's rather more muted defence of Gaullist principles.

In Italy, the foreign policy context has been characterised by an almost complete contrast in attitudes and expectations. These have been aptly and neatly summed up by Pierre Hassner as 'pacifist Atlanticism', indicating both extensive reliance on the political and security dimensions of the Atlantic

---

6 See S. Berger, 'France: Autonomy in Alliance', in D. S. Landes, *op. cit.*, pp. 166-169

framework for determining the shape of Italian foreign policy, and an unwillingness or inability to take significant initiatives either inside or outside this framework. It has been rightly pointed out that a more assertive, independent posture, for example in the Mediterranean area which is of such political, economic and strategic interest to Italy, has been consistently discouraged by the United States in order to avoid upsetting its overall calculations for stability in Southern Europe.[7] Domestic economic and political weaknesses make an Italian bid for a more substantial and unilateral role in foreign policy seem unlikely. At the same time, it is clear that the internal and external reverberations of political changes in Spain and Portugal have begun to make both the Christian Democrat and the Socialist parties reconsider Italy's largely reactive approach to foreign policy. The transition from passive dependency to a more vigorous assertion of Italian interests could take several forms, including resort to a defensive, inward-looking posture as well as attempts to establish bilateral links and develop independent initiatives in areas like the Mediterranean and Middle East to meet specific national needs. The extent to which either is likely depends partly on the prospects for internal political change involving the PCI, but also partly on the evolution of events in Southern Europe and the Mediterranean, which could provide an external justification for sharpening national sensitivities whatever the political composition of the government.

Compared with those of France and Italy, the foreign policy agenda in Spain appears the least fixed and the most open to choices relating to future commitments and objectives. The emergence from the isolation of the Franco period has encouraged more active consideration of foreign policy options, even though the prime focus of political debate has been on the achievement of the transition to internal democracy. This is not to say that there exists a *tabula rasa*. The presence of American military bases in Spain and the 1976 Spanish-American Treaty of Friendship indicate one framework within which fundamental security issues have been partially, if not yet wholly, resolved.[8] In addition, Spain's application for membership of the European Community underlines a concern, reflecting a combination of domestic and external preoccupations, to expand and intensify a variety of links with Western Europe. However, beyond these two commitments of the post-Franco regime, doubts (or simply question marks in view of the possibility of further political change) exist in relation to the extent to which Spain will seek an active involvement in foreign policy. This will turn partly on the way in which Spain's future relationship with the United States is perceived (on both sides). This will either require membership of NATO to provide a fully reciprocal exchange of access to military bases for a defence guarantee, or will be confined to the more

---

[7] S. Berger, 'Italy; on the Threshold or the Brink', in D. S. Landes, *op. cit.*, pp. 232-233.

[8] On this point see A. Sanchez-Gijon, 'Spain and the Atlantic Alliance', *Survival*, Vol. XVIII, 6, November/December, 1976.

limited status of a 'privileged ally'.[9] If the former option is resisted, it may well be the outcome of an attempt to preserve, or more positively develop, some freedom of action. This could be reflected in future Spanish moves to assume the role of an intermediary, in both political and economic terms, between Western Europe and parts of the world such as South America, and even some Arab states, with which the Spanish have claimed a particular affinity.

Given the foreign policy frameworks outlined at the regional level and the contexts for choices at the national levels, is there any correspondence between these and the positions of the PCI, PCF and PCE? This brings us to a closer scrutiny of the parties' foreign policies, particularly those areas where previous attitudes and assumptions have been partially modified, indicating a possible shift in perceptions of national needs and, more broadly, external influences. The parties' positions can be grouped under three headings. The first refers to issues connected with East-West relations, alliance membership and national defence and security commitments arising from these. The second touches on more general foreign policy considerations which impinge on West European interests and potential collaborative activity, while the third involves specifically the North/South dimension. A more complete discussion of the three parties in relation to the European Community can be found in the following chapter.

A fundamental ingredient, indeed the binding agent, in the mix of past assumptions, new expectations, and both short and long term calculations surrounding the Communist parties' analyses of foreign policy has been their interpretation of detente. The influence of detente has already been referred to as a vital factor in shaping the parties' domestic political attitudes. It also has a central role in determining the nature and extent of the re-examination of external commitments and perceptions of security. The linking of detente with particular changes and continuing ambiguities in foreign policy involves three elements. Firstly, for all the parties the ultimate logic of detente requires the dissolution of the two political-military blocs and moves towards an all-European security system, of, as yet, uncertain form. This implies, as it did in a more aggressive climate of Soviet-American relations, no accommodation with NATO or concessions to American security interests in Western Europe, and opposition to the political solidarity projected by the Atlantic Alliance. However, a second element in the interpretation of detente has recently been given greater prominence. For both the PCI and PCE, in particular, longer term objectives have been overlaid by an inclination to define conditions for promoting detente in the more cautious terms of maintaining equilibrium in Europe. Emphasis has shifted from stressing the dynamic element in detente to implying a recognition of an intermediate phase preceding the dissolution of the blocs, in which radical or unilateral disturbance of bloc relations could trigger an international reaction which would, in turn, threaten national goals. Detente, then, has been linked more closely with the existence of a military-

---

9 *Ibid,* p. 253

strategic equilibrium which is directly expressed in the current membership of NATO and the Warsaw Pact. The basic justification put forward for retaining Italian membership of NATO and French participation in the Atlantic Alliance, and for the continuation of American bases in Spain, has been the need to avoid upsetting a rather crudely measured balance. This seems to be a reasonable comment if account is taken of the lower profile which the PCI intends to adopt in NATO, and of the rather different attitudes towards the USA and the USSR which the PCI and PCF might be expected to take compared with the existing 'balance' within the Atlantic Alliance.

The third element links the Communist parties' motives in pursuing detente to their underlying attitudes towards the USSR and the USA and thus to their perceptions of security. Here the overriding impression is one of continuity rather than change, particularly in the regularity with which PCI and PCF leaders have endorsed the Soviet Union's overall objectives and strategy for detente. Thus Georges Marchais' remark, '. . . as far as the problems relating to peaceful co-existence and international detente are concerned we have no criticism to make of Soviet policy,' compares with Berlinguer's equally positive statement; 'We support the fundamental philosophy behind the policy of peaceful co-existence and detente that is being practised by the Soviet Union. But we do not see why this should occasion surprise. It would be irresponsible for us not to recognise what is widely recognised elsewhere, that the Soviet Union's peace is in the general interest of mankind.'[10] The general approbation by the PCI and PCF of the Soviet Union's perception of detente, and their preference for identifying the dangers of imperialist intervention with capitalist states rather than with socialist states, point to fundamental differences over perceptions of security which have yet to be reconciled with the rationale persuading the parties to maintain the formal link with the Atlantic Alliance.

Given the existence of conflicts of interests and loyalties, what kind of role and commitments do the PCI and PCF envisage for themselves within the Atlantic Alliance? Since 1972, the PCF has largely avoided any discussion of the implications of its adherence to the Atlantic Treaty. In view of the differences with the Socialists, particularly before 1976, the PCF preferred to mask its position behind the Common Programme's deliberately vaguely drafted phrase of 'respect for existing alliances.'[11] The one issue on which the party has been clear and emphatic is its refusal to countenance any form of defence collaboration through the NATO structure, or any institutional variant of the kind which has tempted President Giscard d'Estaing's co-operation. Indeed, the foreign policy implications of the party's defence policy suggest only the most tenuous recognition of any form of consultation within the Atlantic framework. It is hard to avoid the conclusion that for the PCF the multilateral dimension of the Atlantic Treaty remains the least developed and perhaps the least desired part of its foreign policy.

---

10 Both quoted in A. Kriegel, *Un Autre Communisme?*, Hachette, Paris, 1977, p. 92.
11 *Programme Commun*, p. 85.

In Italy, by contrast, the closer relationship with the Alliance and the country's military integration into the NATO network created a somewhat different context for the evolution of the position of the PCI. From the end of 1974 onwards, when the PCI dropped its demand for Italian withdrawal from NATO, this aspect of the party's foreign policy was seized on by many observers, either to emphasise changes in its attitudes and assumptions both domestically and internationally, or to underline the party's continuing contradictions and uncertainties in its external role and allegiances. In justifying the reversal of its position and in determining its exact role within the Alliance, the PCI has been engaged in a constant and demanding balancing act. In terms of basic commitment, the party now accepts Italy's membership of NATO, including in principle, if not in detail, the integrated military framework and existence of US bases in Italy. Beyond this, the PCI's view of the external purpose of the Alliance has been guided by two considerations; an unwillingness to concede the existence of a Soviet military threat to Western Europe and an insistence that Italy's involvement in NATO should be limited to defensive needs and, therefore, be territorially restricted. Thus, without advocating full military disengagement, or a formal disavowal of NATO's collective strategic orientation against the USSR, the PCI would nevertheless seek to disassociate Italy from what it regards as the unnecessary or provocative aspects of NATO military doctrine and organisation.[12]

A concern for greater autonomy is carried further in the other part of the PCI's balancing act. This has been directed against American ideological and political penetration of the Atlantic Alliance, and in particular the pre-occupation with domestic stability which the PCI has seen as a threat to internal political change. The party's fundamental and wide-ranging criticism of American domination has posed the problem, both for itself and its potential allies, of the readjustment of intra-Alliance relations which would be necessary to accommodate the PCI's advocacy of a more independent and assertive posture. Thus, 'the whole reason for the attitude of the American rulers lies here; they know, in effect, that the problem is not one of the *guarantees* of an international character which the Communists would have to provide, but rather one of the changes which the Atlantic Pact would have to undergo.'[13] The limits within which the party could envisage any active participation appear to be very narrow. The different strands in the PCI's attempt to find an acceptable modus vivendi with NATO suggest that it could only prevent them from becoming entangled by carefully circumscribing Italy's involvement in both the political and the strategic aspects of the organisation.

By comparison with the PCF, the PCI's rationale for continuing membership of NATO is seen to be bolstered by its recognition of an explicit

---

12 On the whole question of the PCI and NATO see article by Ciro Zoppo, 'The Military Policies of the Italian Communist Party', *Survival,* Vol. XX, March/April, 1978.

13 Alberto Jacoviello, 'The Italian Situation and NATO', *Survival,* Vol. XVIII, 3, May/June, 1976, p. 166.

security interest, touching on its own needs as well as those of Italy. This concerns the strategic and political position of Yugoslavia and the threat it might pose both for Italy and the PCI if the Soviet Union were to take advantage of uncertainty following the death of Tito. References were made during the 1976 election campaign by PCI leaders to the importance of maintaining Yugoslavia's independence.[14] These have been interpreted as indicating the party's awareness of the usefulness of NATO's defence resources in the event of a direct challenge to Yugoslavia, and the possibility of a future Italian Communist government having to work in closer proximity to Soviet influence. Yet the Yugoslav issue also reflects the problems facing the PCI in committing itself to identifying the possibility of a Soviet threat and thereby being associated with what it continues to see as an unnecessarily confrontational stance towards Eastern Europe. One observer has noted that in the debates of the defence committees of the Italian parliament, 'the PCI's major concern has been that Italian military deployments on the north-east borders be greatly reduced lest they seem threatening to Yugoslavia and the Warsaw Pact.'[15]

While going further than the PCF in accepting the basic political and military link between Italy and NATO, the position of the PCI nevertheless suggests continuing tension between its ideological preferences and political resistance to hegemonic tendencies on the one hand, and its fear of upsetting a perceived international equilibrium on the other. The approach of the PCE to NATO falls somewhere between the French and Italian positions. As we have seen, the PCE has declared its willingness to tolerate American bases in Spain so long as comparable military bases, or their equivalent in terms of military links, continue to exist in both Western and Eastern Europe. The party's attitude to NATO, however, takes on shades of a Gaullist-inspired critique, even though Carrillo has committed the party to accepting any vote of a future Spanish parliament in favour of Spain's joining NATO. Thus, 'we think that, above all, NATO is an enormous bureaucracy that tries to perpetuate itself. . . Because in alliances like NATO and the Warsaw Pact, inevitably the strongest power is hegemonic and that irritates—it ends up turning the opinion of the other countries against the power that plays the role. So I, who accept American bases in Spain, don't think it would be useful for Spain to enter NATO.'[16] If Spain were to enter NATO in the future the PCE would find itself in a situation comparable to that of the PCI, to the extent that Spain's strategic and logistic utility, rather than its active military and political contribution to NATO, would form the background against which its relationship with the organisation would, in large part, be measured by the other contributors to NATO's resources.

---

[14] See R. Putman, 'Italian Foreign Policy: Emergent Consensus' in H. R. Penniman, *Italy at the Polls, The Parliamentary Elections of 1976,* Washington, American Enterprise Institute for Public Policy Research, 1977.

[15] C. Zoppa, *op. cit.,* p. 69.

[16] Santiago Carrillo in interview with *New York Times,* January 16, 1977.

The correspondence between the PCI's and PCF's attitudes towards involvement in the Atlantic Alliance and NATO frameworks and their approach to defence policy provides further insights into the factors which have shaped their thinking on external commitments and national priorities. Defence policy has regularly been seen in the past as the leitmotiv of Communist party dependence on the Soviet Union. In the case of the PCF, a shadow has conceivably been cast across this relationship by the party's decision to endorse the French nuclear force. The PCI has appeared to be more concerned with confining the defence profile of Italy to fit with the party's estimate of available economic resources and its more limited assessment of Italy's role within Europe and particularly the Mediterranean area. There has been no equivalent dramatic gesture in the PCI's focus on defence policy to compare with the reversal of its opposition to NATO.[17] Although the party has long campaigned for a reduction in Italy's defence budget, it has nevertheless not opposed the progressive reorganisation and modernisation of the Italian armed forces and has tended, more recently, to emphasise the necessity for greater cost-effectiveness in scrutinising military expenditure. This latter approach has been suggested as one explanation for the participation of PCI deputies in the discussions of the Armaments Commission of Western European Union in the spring of 1977, and their willingness to agree to proposals for standardisation of weapons production within Western Europe. The major part of the PCI's attempt to alter the direction of national defence policy has concentrated on advocating greater democracy within the structure of Italy's armed forces and, especially, the need to bring the whole military sector under closer parliamentary control. While the party would probably underline the importance of such moves to its domestic political reform programme, they would nevertheless reinforce the PCI's concern to limit the subordination of Italian defence practices and doctrines to a suspected NATO-inspired set of priorities.

In contrast to the PCI, the PCF has made its major gesture of change in its overall foreign policy approach in the area of defence policy. The Central Committee's endorsement of the French nuclear force in May 1977, after some months of hints from individual party leaders, led to both inter-party and apparently intra-party debate concerning the coherence and direction of the party's foreign and defence policies.[18] The PCF's conversion to the principle of nuclear deterrence as the basis of French security has been repeatedly justified by Marchais and Jean Kanapa, the PCF foreign affairs spokesman, on the grounds of the party's reluctant acknowledgement of the excessive reliance of French defence on the nuclear weapon and, secondly, the contribution of a major deterrent capacity to French military and political independence. It became clear in the debates in 1977 between the PCF and the Socialists that the former were prepared to accept the full range of weapons making up the

---

[17] C. Zoppa, *op. cit.,* pp. 65-66 and p. 70 on which this paragraph draws heavily.
[18] See *Le Monde,* 13 May; 27 May; 8 June; 17 June; 22 June, 1977.

nuclear force. The PCF's attitude to the maintenance and further development of the force, although not spelled out clearly, has appeared to go beyond the position of its would-be Socialist coalition partners. 'We are in favour of maintaining (the nuclear force) at the minimum level required by the demands of security and French independence.'[19]

The party's identification with an aspect of French defence policy, which it previously vigorously condemned, has been made not without cost to its traditional critical stance, nor indeed to the efficacy and acceptability of its nuclear strategy *vis-à-vis* external threats. Given the PCF's criticism of the lack of democracy in the military sector, it has faced a difficult problem justifying the inevitable concentration of decison making associated with the management of nuclear weaponry. The quid pro quo of the PCF's acceptance of the nuclear force has been its insistence on strict adherence to the strategy of 'tous azimuts' in the weapon's targeting and the warning that, in pursuit of its strictly independent and neutral approach to defining threats to French security, it would end any informal French participation in the communications and early-warning network within the Atlantic framework. Both aspects have been seized on by the PCF's opponents and sceptics to question the lack of credibility in the basic deterrent value of the force if such a rigorous interpretation of independence was to be adopted. One clearly unimpressed commentator, in the light of the party's emphasis on distinguishing its nuclear strategy from any association with a pro-NATO orientation has wrily noted that it resembles 'the logic of Jokari; whatever the subtlety of presentation, it always comes back to the Kremlin.'[20]

From the point of view of the PCF, the role and integration of its new commitment to the French nuclear force in the party's overall foreign policy would depend, in a future Left government, on the pace of a re-organisation of the conventional armed forces and its expectations concerning further progress towards general nuclear disarmament. The party has, so far, appeared to keep the problem of the consistency of its fundamental attitude towards the nuclear force at arms length by essentially presenting its conversion as a stop-gap measure. It is, nevertheless, one which, when considered along with the party's limited tolerance of France's adherence to the Atlantic Treaty, provides a significant indicator of its continuing reluctance to concede, or willingness to exploit, the principle and the resources of French independence.

A consequence of the approach of both the PCI and PCF to national defence policy, though possibly less true of the PCE, is a refusal to countenance any form of active European defence collaboration, even if developed as an alternative to excessive military dependence on the United States. Without the involvement, or, as they see it, interference of the United States there remains a major obstacle, in the shape of the parties' attitudes to

---

[19] Jean Kanapa, quoted from interview on French television in *L'Humanité*, 27 July, 1977.

[20] P. Wajsman in *Le Figaro*, 9 September, 1977.

West Germany, which not only rules out defence co-operation but also conceivably raises the question of their basic acceptance of the Atlantic Alliance. Co-existence of this acceptance with persistent criticism of West German economic and political motives and the frequent condemnation of an alleged American-West German hegemony over Western Europe have been continuing features of the positions of the PCI and PCF. Of the two the PCF has been the most vociferous in repudiating any defence link with West Germany, including taking the line, in its advocacy of a purely national deterrent strategy, of opposing French commitment to a forward battle on German territory. The parties' hostility or suspicion towards West Germany, and indeed, their reluctance to regard the USSR as a threat to security, pose problems for any observer attempting to project responses to future crises. Doubts, particularly in the minds of American and West German decision-makers about the effects of residual anti-Germanism on the 'reliability' of the PCI and PCF in the event of a threat to West Germany certainly exist. In the absence of such a threat, the West German factor renders any 'Europeanising' of Atlantic relations an unacceptable alternative to the adoption of a low national profile by the PCF and PCI as the corollary of their condemnation of excessive American influence over the Atlantic Alliance.

It is worth noting the reactions of the PCI, PCF and PCE to one major defence issue raised by the USA within the Atlantic framework during 1978 which not only united the three parties but also indicated their residual identification with the views and leadership of the USSR. The possible development of the neutron bomb and its deployment by the Americans in Western Europe, in particular in West Germany, sparked off a concerted campaign in the West European Communist parties reminiscent of their earlier denunciations of NATO. The issue was a 'safe' one as far as the Communist parties were concerned; it neatly combined the targets of anti-Americanism, anti-militarism and opposition to any disturbance of the existing strategic balance in Europe. Indeed, this was one issue on which the PCI preferred to associate itself with a collective condemnation of the neutron bomb drawn up by the international Communist movement, under the guidance of the USSR, rather than seek to exercise any independent initiative.

Toleration of the mechanisms and commitments implied in the Alliance framework, then, clearly has its limits. This is demonstrated further in the preference of the parties for safeguarding and, where possible, extending national initiatives in the wider context of East-West relations in Europe. The expectation that the CSCE process will lay the foundations for superceding the two blocs has reinforced the PCI's policy of stressing the need for more active Italian diplomacy *vis-à-vis* relations with East European states. While this theme has been a traditional feature of Communist party criticisms of bloc-imposed priorities in the conduct of East-West relations, the principles and momentum associated with the CSCE have provided the PCI with an additional argument, or alternative rationale, in favour of developing a more independent policy. Nor has the party been slow to invoke the principles of the

Helsinki final act to justify its resistance to what are seen as unacceptable features of bloc relations in Western Europe, including the question of the locating of tactical nuclear weapons on Italian soil and the right to determine control over foreign military bases.

Another specific issue on which the parties have chosen to question the appropriateness and priorities of the Alliance framework has been the achievement of progress in disarmament negotiations in Europe. Here the pace has been set, not surprisingly, by the PCF. The latter, in support of its position in favour of French participation in the MBFR (Mutual Balanced Force Reductions) talks has drawn the opposite conclusion to that of the French Government in advocating French involvement precisely to challenge the principle that the talks on force reductions are the preserve of the two blocs. Furthermore, the party has expressed its determination not to allow France's adherence to the Atlantic Alliance to subject any future Left government initiative on disarmament or force reductions to a 'blocage atlantique'.[21]

The focus so far has been largely on changes and readjustments in the positions of the PCI, PCF and PCE which have involved compromises on past principles and a re-examination of previous assumptions. The wider foreign policy reverberations of these concessions made in response to the perceived requirements of continued international detente and national political objectives, remain uncertain. This is so, not least because they coexist with attitudes and policies which suggest a different and potentially conflicting set of foreign policy preferences to those currently expounded within the Atlantic or West European frameworks. We noted earlier that most observers have emphasised the continuing pro-Soviet orientation of the foreign policies of the PCI, PCF and PCE. This has been generally measured in terms of the identification of the parties with the view that international relations involve competition and confrontation between the forces of imperialism and socialism. Thus, Annie Kriegel, one of the leading French experts on the PCF, concluded from the report on foreign affairs presented by Jean Kanapa to the PCF's Central Committee in May, 1976 that in none of the nineteen areas discussed was there any indication of a party view significantly different from that of the Soviet Union.[22] The main issues on which the three parties have consistently criticised Western attitudes have been those where American and West European motives have been mistrusted, or where ideological sympathies have encouraged the espousal of liberation movements. Prominent examples are the strong support given by the PCI, PCF and PCE to the Palestinian cause in the Middle East and their responses to intervention and conflict in Africa. Whether or not it is accepted as a matter of course that solidarity with the USSR is the principal stimulus determing the parties' foreign policy reflexes, it seems clear that the commitment to 'struggles against imperialism' and alternative definitions of foreign policy interests imply a re-examination

---

[21] Jean Kanapa, *Le Monde Diplomatique*, March 1977. See also PCF memorandum on disarmament, May 1978.

[22] A. Kriegel, *op. cit.*, p. 92.

of existing international relationships. Such an examination is unlikely to be totally undermined by further assertions of independence from the Soviet Union. In other words, should the PCI, PCF or PCE enter government, their influence may well lead to a shift of emphasis and a more radical direction for national foreign policies. The extent to which these shifts will occur and affect the climate for foreign policy consensus in Western Europe will depend, in part, on the overall political composition and priorities of future Left governments and, not least, on the Communist parties' willingness and capacity to commit themselves to initiatives of substance as distinct from rhetorical gestures.

Apart from attitudes towards basic security issues already discussed in relation to links with NATO and the Atlantic Alliance, the underlying foreign policy assumptions of the PCI, PCF and PCE point to a sharpened confrontation with existing national and collective West European postures, particularly *vis-à-vis* the Third World. Although these differences would inevitably impinge to some extent on Alliance relationships and attitudes towards the United States, they are likely to affect positions and issues more immediately within the narrower context of Western Europe. In terms both of general stance and responses to specific events, the political co-operation procedure of the European Community would conceivably feel some reverberations from greater influence of the Communist parties in government, and further pressure on the existing, often tenuous capacity for the definition of common interests. The parties' attitudes towards foreign policy collaboration within the Community framework are not really separable from their overall responses to the European Community which are considered at greater length in the following chapter. However, it is worth noting at this point the relationship between the parties' foreign policy preferences and those which have so far been debated via the political co-operation procedure, if only because the latter would represent a further criterion by which independence and assertiveness in foreign policy would be judged. Neither the PCI nor the PCF has indicated precisely what position it would adopt in principle towards involvement in Community foreign policy consultations. If it is assumed (in the light of their adherence to the rest of the Community framework), that there will be no outright opposition, and given the relative flexibility and absence of pressures to reach binding agreements characteristic of these consultations, the parties' responses would probably be determined by particular issues. There are three areas involving some degree of collective West European interest, where the current emphasis and approach of the PCI, PCF and PCE would pose problems in attempts to evolve a common policy or take a more active initiative at the European level.

Firstly, in the Middle East, in so far as the PCI, PCF and PCE have advocated the assertion of Palestinian rights in opposition to Israeli claims and have suspected the motives for excluding Soviet involvement in peace moves as a result of the American-Egyptian rapprochement, their consequent identification with Soviet interests would challenge the cautious balancing act which the European Community has hitherto tried (albeit not very actively or successfully) to adopt. In economic terms, it is less clear whether the Communist parties would be prepared to resist multilateral initiatives like the Euro-Arab dialogue, or challenge the evaluation of politico-economic interests involved, by preferring to substitute bilateral links which would reflect particular national priorities. In this case, the attitudes of the Arab States themselves could play a significant role.

A second area, concerns disputes over outside intervention in internal conflict, especially in Africa, where attemps by the European Community to achieve a degree of diplomatic unity would be further complicated by more radical interpretations of the interests at stake. Here, the importance of the potential differences between, for example, Italian and French Governments with PCI and PCF representation, and their Community partners would turn on the extent to which PCI and PCF verbal support for examples of 'fraternal assistance' to liberation movements would be converted into more concrete aid. Although the latter is unlikely, PCI and PCF endorsement of the Cuban and Soviet role in Southern Africa would add a more pronounced ideological twist to the disagreements over the extent of, and motives for, involvement in internal conflict, revealed in the Community's disarray over French and Belgian participation in Zaire. Projection of future Communist reaction to further outside intervention in intra-African conflict is made more hazardous given the emergence of some reservations on the part of the PCI and, more recently, the PCF, over Soviet policy in the Ethiopian-Somalian dispute. The PCI, apparently embarrassed by the Soviet Union's tilt towards the Ethiopians at the expense of Somalia, was the first to indicate its doubts about the consequences of Soviet-backed Cuban involvement in the Horn of Africa. Subsequently the PCF, by the spring of 1978, was beginning to voice concern about the naked use of force, reinforced by external intervention, in disputes involving two anti-imperialist African states.

Thirdly, an interesting combination of internal and external preoccupation with the scope and consequences of political change suggest that the question of Mediterranean security and stability would provide room for mutual suspicion, if not conflict, between governments containing the PCI, PCF and PCE on the one hand, and wary social democratic or right of centre governments on the other. In terms of shaping internal political change, the collective West European reaction to events in Portugal in 1975 reflected a common desire to weaken the position of the Portuguese Communist party. Although the PCI and PCE were critical of the Portuguese party's strategy at the time, they and the PCF could not be expected to endorse any future reaction of a similar kind which would be so overtly aimed at asserting a Community interest in the area at the expense of a fellow Communist party.

In the absence of any 'teeth' to the Community's foreign policy consultation procedure and the uncertainty surrounding the extent of active involvement of future governments of the Left in those areas impinging on shared West European interests, it would be unwise to regard the procedure as presenting

56

any kind of fundamental constraint against a reorientation of foreign policy. Moreover, and in more human terms, given the emphasis on the use of the political co-operation procedure primarily as an information and deliberative network, much would depend on the attitudes and expectations of other governments and, not least, the actual presence of a PCF or PCI foreign minister and the approaches and assumptions of their officials.

Finally, to complete the picture of the Communist parties' alternative conceptions of foreign policy interests and strategies in the wider international context, mention should also be made of their approach to the issues raised in the North/South dialogue between developed and developing countries. Here, the extent of competition or reconciliation with existing attitudes and policies turns partly on the analysis of international economic factors, which are seen to be responsible for the impoverishment of developing countries, and partly on the mechanisms and frameworks through which a more equitable redistribution of resources could be achieved. The major emphasis, which characterises all three parties' approach to North/South issues, lies in underlining the role of multinational companies as the main agents in depressing the income and reinforcing the dependence of developing countries in relation to the needs and priorities of industrialised producers and consumers. Both the PCI and the PCF have advocated the negotiation of long term bilateral agreements between future governments of the Left and raw materials producers as a more effective way of stabilising producer returns.[23] From the parties' point of view, such State to State agreements would bypass and reduce the role of multinational companies, while assuring stable supplies to Italy and France as a result of the establishment of what are presumed will be more sympathetic political and economic relationships. How far such expectations would be realised would clearly depend on the future priorities of the raw material producers themselves, and the domestic economic programmes of governments with PCI and PCF representation. By comparison with the PCI and PCE, the PCF has been the most concerned to assert its independence of any bloc ties in the development of proposals for reform of the international economic order. It has been especially critical of multilateral frameworks such as the European Community and the Conference on International Economic Co-operation on the grounds that they reflect only a cross section of the political and economic interests necessary for transforming the basis of relations between developed and developing countries. Arguably, the differences in approach and policies among the PCI, PCF and PCE and their potential West European partners (who disagree already in their assessments of Third World problems) on questions connected with the North/South dialogue, would turn less on their diplomatic dependence on the Soviet Union than on rival economic interpretations of the issues involved and the scope for generosity.

---

[23] See speech by Georges Marchais on proposals for a new international economic order in Mexico, 16 May, 1978 published in *Les Communistes Français et L'Europe*, No. 2, June 1978, pp. 35-37.

The spectrum of issues and general foreign policy orientations outlined so far indicate the international framework within which the parties have sought to take up a more appropriate and flexible position to correspond with their domestic preoccupations. The underlying point which emerges repeatedly from discussions of the foreign policy positions of the PCI, PCF and PCE is the unresolved tension, or, less charitably, the outright contradiction between the parties' attempts to deal pragmatically with bloc politics and the assumptions and objectives which are part of their ideological and political baggage as Communist parties. So far they have seen the problem of balancing these conflicting elements in their foreign policy strategies in two ways. Firstly, at the regional level, the parties have set out to compensate for their concessions to the existence of the blocs by narrowly circumscribing their accommodation with the Atlantic Alliance, and by taking up a vigorously critical stance towards American influence in Western Euope. Secondly, they have emphasised particular national needs and international goals which require more independent and assertive policies at the national level.

On both levels, the effects of the PCF's approach on French positions would be generally to reinforce and further sharpen, rather than dramatically change, the pre-Giscard d'Estaing assumptions and direction of French policy, particularly *vis-à-vis* European-American relations and the safeguarding of French independence. (One major exception where the PCF has felt no need to make concessions on the grounds of maintaining an 'international eqilibrium', and where its highly critical attitude would certainly provoke a fundamental break, concerns French involvement in African affairs.) By contrast, the PCI's stance would have the effect of directly challenging Italy's normally compliant role at the regional level, while introducing a much more overtly independent and active dimension into Italian foreign policy at the national level. Although less explicit, the PCE's overall approach to foreign policy would seem to point both to the adoption of a more active defence of Spanish interests in the sense of rejecting de facto dependence on the United States and, at the same time, the exploitation of West European links where these could be shown to bring greater resources to bear, particularly on North/South issues.

It follows from what has been said already that there is at least some correspondence between the critical themes which the three parties have emphasised in their responses to Atlantic and European diplomatic issues and the common concerns, at both the national and international level, of existing governments. To some extent, this narrows the gap between the positions currently adopted by governments of the Right and Centre-Left and the alternatives proposed by the Communist parties. At the same time, it is misleading to see the PCI, PCF and PCE as posing a uniform challenge to the political status quo or committed to identical perspectives and priorities. On defence and security matters and, indeed, in the manner of their projection of foreign policy issues, the differences are striking. It is clear that the parties have given greater thought to the limited number of questions, such as Atlantic relations and defence roles, on which they have been prepared to outline their policies in some detail. On other issues, such as North/South relations or more geographically distant and ideologically divisive areas, the parties have either fallen back on an endorsement of positions coincident with Soviet interests and interpretations, or have groped hesitatingly towards expressing reservations of Soviet tactics, if not what are deemed to be the ultimate Soviet goals. Overall, and seen primarily from an international perspective, the parties' foreign policies pose problems of both internal consistency and external uncertainty.

V Autonomy and Interdependence: the Issue of the EEC

The issues of NATO membership, Alliance commitments and security perceptions have provided one set of criteria for assessing the external implications of the changes in the domestic strategy and increased political influence of the PCI, PCF and PCE. The other commonly used measure has involved attitudes and policies towards the European Community. The latter are taken to represent an amalgam of political and economic issues including, in the narrowest sense, observance of existing international obligations by the three parties when in government, and in the widest sense, their recognition, tolerance and even exploitation of international economic interdependence.

The Communist parties' reactions to the European Community can be seen as one indicator of the relations envisaged between future socialist economies and external economic interests and pressures. On a number of the foreign policy issues already discussed, the PCI, PCF and PCE have been able to defer awkward choices into the more distant future, on the basis of a reasonable confidence in the continuation of detente and an anticipation that their West European potential allies and the USA would accept their presence in government. However, they have been under somewhat greater pressure, from both political rivals and outsiders, to declare their hands *vis-à-vis* the range of international arenas and interests with which the economies of Italy, France and Spain are involved. The possibility of confrontation has been threatened or hinted at on both sides. Redistributive and potentially protectionist and inward-looking policies have been advocated with varying degrees of aggressiveness by the Communist parties. In response, plans to withdraw investment, credit and sympathy appear to have been at least contemplated by the United States and West Germany and by the European Community.

At the same time it is arguable that the rhythm and interlocking nature of economic and industrial growth in Western Europe, and the increasing difficulties of independent domestic economic management, have combined to raise the cost of radical changes in national economic policies. An increase in the costs incurred does not mean that such changes are inconceivable. It nevertheless poses, for countries like Italy and France especially, some difficult choices between, on the one hand, accepting both the buffeting and the support of international economic interests and, on the other, searching for a more controllable but possibly less prosperous national economic strategy. These factors appear to have influenced, though by no means totally undermined, the framework within which the PCI, PCF and PCE have come to consider their plans for the transition to a socialist economy, and to assess the political and economic consequences of external repercussions which might follow a sudden repudiation of international economic links.

Many of the warnings and misgivings which emerged in response to the PCI's and PCF's increased political strength between 1976 and 1978 concerned both the dangers and constraints involved in fitting socialist economic policies into the trade, investment and international financial framework of Western Europe. Thus the importance of foreign trade to the structure and wealth of the French and Italian economies has been seen as a major factor restricting the room for manoeuvre in external economic policy. In terms of international capital investment and the contribution of multinational companies to production and technological development in certain industrial sectors, France and, more especially, Italy and Spain, are significantly vulnerable to fears aroused by the prospect of more punitive policies on taxation, industrial ownership and the movement of capital. Since the oil crisis in 1973 and the inflationary consequences and balance of payments difficulties which followed in its wake, major oil-importing countries like France and Italy have either (as in the case of Italy), become more dependent on various forms of international credit to overcome periods of severe trade and payment imbalances, or found domestic economic directives increasingly overtaken by more clamorous external demands.[1]

How far are these features of economic interdependence in Western Europe seen both by the parties themselves and by outsiders as unavoidable constraints inhibiting any fundamental change of direction in national economic policy? There are two principal ways in which the potential impact of the PCI, PCF and PCE on this network of international economic relations can be examined in the context of the parties' domestic economic and political strategies and their future priorities, if they were to enter government. The first is the most conjectural and therefore, less amenable to any firm conclusions in advance, without information on the domestic conditions under which the parties might assume office. In addition, the political identity and policies of their likely coalition partners would be important factors. It raises the question of the overall external impact of domestic economic policies designed to redistribute wealth more evenly, to control 'market forces' more vigorously and to increase the level of public expenditure. Much speculation has gone into the possibility that pressure from the PCI, or the PCF within a future Union of the Left, would lead to government policies which would bring about a rapid rise in inflation, and trigger an economic crisis which would necessitate the involvement of international institutions and external

---

[1]These points have been discussed in more detail in unpublished papers by R. Lieber and W. Goldstein prepared for an International Seminar on Foreign Policy and the West European Left held at Columbia University, New York, June 27-28, 1977.

financial support in the maintenance of domestic economies. The prospect of such a clash depends, in part, on the second, more specific aspect of the parties' anticipated impact on international economic relations. This concerns their attitudes towards continuing, or reducing to a minimum, the 'openness' of national economies to external interests via trade, investment flows and responses to multinational business activities.

If the parties' current positions are taken at face value there is a clear difference in emphasis and approach between the PCE and PCI on the one hand, and the PCF on the other. Both the PCE and PCI have indicated their awareness of, and willingness to endorse, the extent of their countries' dependence on direct foreign investment and trade flows to sustain further economic growth.[2] In the case of the PCI this has led to the suggestion that controls against the unacceptable features of multinational companies should be imposed via the European Community rather than ineffectually, and in a particularly costly manner, by Italy acting alone. Moreover, the PCI has appeared to rule out any major policy of unilateral import restrictions and imposition of blanket protectionist measures as a means of overcoming the imbalances in the Italian economy (while reserving the right to follow existing government practice by introducing partial and temporary measures).[3]

The impression given by the PCF, both in the party's domestic economic programme and in its attitude towards external links and interests, is one of much sharper confrontation with the assumptions and policies of an 'open' economy. The party's differences with the Socialists over the Common Programme in 1977, particularly the extent and means by which major private companies would be nationalised, indicate the PCF's determination to make a radical break with the structures and symbols of a capitalist economy, implying tighter regulation of internal and external economic activity. In terms of external measures the PCF's argument has been that trade, financial and other economic controls could not be abandoned as instruments for curbing the unacceptable influence of international capital over the French economy, or for preventing disruptions or threats to the implementation of the socialist programme. This does not amount to a complete surrender to autarkic principles. Indeed, the party has acknowledged the need to maintain certain trade links in the interests of further economic growth. It does, however, suggest a radical change of priorities, and a readiness to assert the claims of domestic objectives should these conflict with the rules or requirements of international economic institutions.

From the evidence so far, the PCE and PCI appear far less inclined to provoke a sudden or fundamental reversal of existing ties with the international economy, both in their pursuit of domestic economic reform and in an apparent recognition of the dependence of Spain and Italy on external

[2]On this point see analysis by R. Putnam, 'Interdependence and the Italian Communists', *International Organisation,* Spring, 1978.

[3]See the Report on the Economy of CESPE (Centro di Studi di politica economica del PCI) published in D. Sasson (ed.), *The Italian Communists Speak for Themselves,* Spokesman, 1978.

markets, supplies and investment. The PCF's position is likely to be much less accommodating depending on its strength in a future coalition with the Socialists, and the influence over the latter of the CERES group's preference for promoting French self-sufficiency. The party's presence in government would provoke a rigorous scrutiny of the terms, conditions and necessity for external penetration of the French economy.

The two basic issues raised so far concerning the perceived constraints imposed by interdependence and reliance on international institutions and external assistance in the event of an economic crisis are both entwined in the parties' attitudes towards the European Community. The latter, because of the intensity of the economic ties involved and the closeness of political and institutional links, presents problems for the choice between autonomy and interdependence in a most immediate and acute form. Before examining the parties' attempts to come to terms with these problems within the Community framework, it is worth noting some further aspects of the relationship between the European Community and the overall political approach of the three parties.

By comparison with other foreign policy questions, that of the European Community reflects a more complex network of issues combining domestic and external, economic and political elements which appear to touch on the revised strategies of the PCI, PCF and PCE at several points. One interesting feature of changing party reactions has been the tendency to distinguish membership of the European Community from other foreign policy areas and in particular, from previous association with the objectives of United States foreign policy. This less uncompromisingly critical approach to European integration is illustrated in the moves which the PCI and PCE have made towards incorporating and exploiting the regional dimension in their domestic strategies, as well as envisaging the Community as a vehicle for strengthening Western Europe's autonomy in a wider international sense. The PCF's interpretation of the contribution and potential of a suitably reformed European Community to its internal and external goals is much more heavily circumscribed. Nevertheless, even the PCF's strictly limited approach is an indication of its preparedness to separate the Community from a previously tightly-integrated set of responses in foreign policy.

One of the advantages in taking the European Community as a field in which to explore the extent of the parties' modifications in attitudes and policies is that the Community encompasses issues involving both external loyalties and objectives, and internal political and economic profiles. In other words, the Community represents one arena where the foreign policy positions and domestic political images of the parties come together in close proximity. For this reason, the European Community has sometimes been taken (perhaps not very appropriately) as a 'litmus test' of the independence of the Communist parties, their willingness to subscribe to 'bourgeois' political rules and institutions 'beyond the nation state' and their commitment to a peaceful road to socialism.

From the point of view of the Communist parties themselves, Community issues arguably provide a more direct and tangible set of questions than a number of other foreign policy areas on which to project alternative strategies and from which some electoral impact and return might be anticipated. It is evident from the substance and the political procedures involved in European Community issues that they belong to neither exclusively foreign nor exclusively domestic policy categories. The large degree of overlap which exists has increasingly demanded an extension to the normal arena for political activity. So many areas impinge on the domestic politics of the Member States that any political party seeking to win power cannot afford to ignore this extra dimension of political competition. This was conceded by the PCI from the early 1960s and led to its campaign for representation in the European Parliament to advance the interests of Italian workers, in recognition of the political and economic significance of the Community for Italian economic growth. The PCF's conversion to this view was inhibited by the party's more determined opposition to the political superstructure of the Community, and the French Government's persistent refusal in the 1960s to endorse PCF representation in the French delegation to the European Parliament. However, since 1973, not only has the PCF joined the PCI to create a joint parliamentary group, but it has more recently begun to exploit in the domestic arena the political capital gained from exposure of Community inadequacy in a range of policy sectors.[4]

In terms of domestic importance, major areas of Community activity, especially the Common Agricultural Policy, the Community's contribution to industrial, social and regional policies, and attempts to co-ordinate the overall management of national economic policies, provide highly appropriate campaign issues. The prospect of a further enlargement of the European Community which would add the claims of three relatively poor Mediterranean countries to the demands on scarce resources has made substantial inroads into domestic politics in Italy and France. Since the European Community does, to some extent, affect the distribution of wealth both within and between member countries, it offers both protection and threats to those social and economic interests with which the Communist parties in France, Italy and Spain have identified themselves. The greater exposure of the positions of PCI and PCF in relation to the European Community as a result of the first round of direct elections to the European Parliament in 1979, both *vis-à-vis* the electorate and other political parties, has contributed an extra element of competition and a further opportunity to test their political support in this part of the political arena.

The success with which the three Communist parties have been able to exploit specific Community questions in the quest for greater political legitimacy has, of course, depended on the reconciliation of the existence and

---

[4]For documentary evidence of this campaigning interest in the European Community see issues of *Les Communistes Francais et L'Europe* produced by the PCF's delegation to the European Parliament.

objectives of the European Community with their underlying political and economic assumptions. To the extent that the European Community and the Atlantic Alliance were for so long bracketed together by the USSR as the twin arms of capitalism and imperialism, toleration of both has not merely involved the parties in differences with the Soviet Union, but also in a political reassessment of the mechanisms and dynamics of relations among West European States. In an economic sense, the principles and policy implications of European integration have been seen, in the past, as posing a basic challenge to the achievement of a socialist economy. In what ways, then, have the PCF, PCI and PCE come to terms with the European Community? How far do their positions illustrate a common reorientation of political and economic strategies or, conversely, confirm the differences and reservations noted in the proceding chapter in relation to other foreign policy issues? The parties' responses can be divided into three areas; their attitudes to the fundamental economic ideology and rationale of the European Community, to the Community institutional framework and to specific policy objectives and priorities.

Compared with the adjustment of the PCI, PCF and PCE to the rationale and justification supporting the Atlantic Alliance, their partial acknowledgement of the economic rationale behind the European Community has developed over a longer period and, for the PCI and PCE, been more closely attuned to perceptions of domestic needs. In the case of the PCI, its accommodation with the Community dates from the early 1960s and was one of the factors in the party's reconsideration of both its domestic and international alliances.[5] The PCE and PCF have followed the PCI at a somewhat slower pace, although the PCE now seems to share the PCI's readiness to envisage a central role for the European Community in the management of international economic relations. The PCF, on the other hand, appears to have run into more difficulty in integrating its acceptance of the Community in the 1972 Common Programme into the rest of its analysis of international capitalism. It would be an exaggeration to argue that the Communist parties' attempts to make room in their ideological frameworks for the economic processes reflected in the European Community have pushed them towards a fully-developed counter-ideology for European integration. The process of ideological adjustment has been a much more limited exercise. It has been confined primarily to opposing the explicitly capitalist philosophy contained in the Rome Treaty, and to attempting a socialist justification for the maintenance of the basic common market principles of freer trade, mobility of capital, and other factors of production. The retreat from the Soviet position of relegating the economic significance of the European Community to a subordinate place was begun by the PCI in its analysis of the dynamics of Italy's post-war internal and external economic development. Italy set the pace and the USSR and the rest of the international Communist movement

---

[5]See D. Blackmer, *Unity in Diversity: Italian Communism and Communist World*, MIT Press, 1968, Chapter 9.

accorded the European Community a more respectable status and greater permanency in 1962, seeing it as 'a new phenomenon in the development of the capitalist economy, arising from an objective economic need to create larger markets and greater international specialisation of production.'[6]

The PCI has since gone further in its assessment of the depth and implications of the process of economic integration. It has contended that the process is not only irreversible but could be adapted for progressive ends, given its challenge to outmoded forms of production based on irrelevant and discriminatory national boundaries. Such a technocratic analysis is tempered by the party's political reservations concerning the Community's present institutional balance and representation of political forces which, in its view, perpetuate the capitalist exploitation of the larger market.

Given the comments made earlier about the PCF's general conception of the link between socialist economic policies and external economic interests, it is not surprising that the party has found few positive features to explore in the Community's economic framework. Almost all the party's general economic references to the processes of European integration reflect a highly sceptical view of their contribution to economic welfare. They are seen principally as offering sustenance to the influence and control of multinational companies. While note is taken of the increasing 'internationalisation' of the economy, and the need to exploit new production techniques and take advantage of pooled resources to develop major industrial projects, all of which militate against any lapse into autarky, the PCF, nevertheless, insists on the maintenance of national independence as a vital factor in the battle against international capitalism.[7] This scarcely leaves any room for a rapprochement with the PCI's anticipation of potential socialist adaptation of the Community framework. However the PCF has joined with the PCI and PCE in pressing for maximising the representation of workers' interests within the Community framework. It is clear from the continuing criticisms which the parties have made of the Community's encouragement to free market forces that they remain suspicious of the economic rationale involved in integration. Nevertheless, the PCI and PCE would appear to find sufficient justification in the increasing transnational scope of economic activity to warrant the exploitation of the Community's potential regulatory powers in this area. It is much less certain from the PCF's statements with what degree of enthusiasm, and under what kind of circumstances, it would be prepared to envisage a similar Community role.

If the economic assumptions underpinning the European Community have proved contentious, the political superstructure has presented a further challenge both to the parties' traditional reflexes and to their efforts to alter their domestic political images. Although the supranational features of the Community institutions were partly responsible for the Communist parties'

6Quoted in D. Blackmer, *ibid.,* p. 316.

7See points made in introductory speech by Gustave Ansart, leader of first PCF delegation to European Parliament in 1973.

repudiation of the whole Community framework in the 1950s and 1960s, the evolution of the PCI's views and the differences between the PCI and the PCF over the direct election and powers of the European Parliament have revealed interesting divergencies of opinion. The PCF has consistently and vehemently rejected all supranational aspects of the Community institutions as an affront to the basic principle of national sovereignty. The party has reserved its sharpest and most potent criticism for the Commission and the European Parliament. The Commission is treated not so much with disdain in the Gaullist tradition, as inextricably identified with the interests of exploitative economic forces, for whose benefit it attempts to rationalise markets (as in coal and steel) and open up new areas for the penetration of European capital (as in the conclusion of the Lomé Convention).[8] The PCF has staunchly defended the maintenance of the veto in the Council of Ministers. Its representatives in the party's delegation to the European Parliament have regularly fallen back on affirming the rather uncertain principle that only from a position of real and substantial independence can any Member State envisage co-operation with its Community partners.

By contrast, the PCI's institutional approach appears much more flexible. Indeed, its emphases and criticisms are developed in a strikingly opposite direction to those of the PCF. Far from rejecting the status and role of the Commission, the party has advocated a restoration of the institutional balance in order to revive its basic political function. The PCI has aimed its most effective ammunition at the Council of Ministers and, more recently, the European Council (the regular 'summit' meetings of the Heads of State and Governments of the Nine), for keeping decision making in the hands of unrepresentative groups and being open to manipulation by the more powerful governments at the expense of weaker countries. As Don Sassoon has rightly noted, this suspicion and criticism of the Council of Ministers provides an interesting contrast with the views of opponents on the Left in Britain of the respective roles of the Council and Commission in the European Community.[9] It is worth recalling, in the light of the parties' attitudes in the NATO context, that a recurring theme in both the French and the Italian responses to the Community framework has been the influence and objectives of West Germany and its political and economic significance in the integration process. Paradoxically, the two parties have reached opposite conclusions on the institutional implications of this alleged 'threat'. Fear of West German dominance has further encouraged the PCI to campaign against the central role of the Council of Ministers and inter-governmental procedures on the grounds that they provide West Germany with a major channel for influencing the direction and priorities of the Community (as the PCI pointed out in relation to the German initiative over the European Monetary System). On the other hand, the PCF has stressed the need to rely on the Council of Ministers

---

[8] A multilateral trade and aid agreement signed in 1975 between the European Community and over 50 African, Caribbean and Pacific States.

[9] D. Sassoon, *op. cit.*, p. 41, footnote 118.

exercising appropriate control over the Commission, as long as the latter maintains its claims to supranationalism which the PCF considers as a veiled mechanism for the assertion of German economic ascendancy.

Finally, the emergence of the issue of direct elections to the European Parliament on to the centre of the Community's political stage, and as a significant domestic political question in France, has presented the parties with a further opportunity (or possibly an embarrassing occasion) for confronting their differing conceptions of political authority and objectives within the European Community. For the PCI, the issue not only presents no problems in terms of its response or commitment, but satisfies one of the party's long-standing goals in relation to the democratisation of Community institutions and processes.[10] The party's support for direct elections goes back to 1969 and its first appearance in the European Parliament. It has advocated direct elections not merely as a method for redressing the Parliament's status *vis-à-vis* the other institutions but, more generally, as a way of broadening the mobilisation of support for political and economic change on to the regional level. Thus, the direct election of the Parliament, particularly if conducted under a system of proportional representation in every Member State, would strengthen the representation of socialists and 'democratic and progressive' forces within the Community and contribute to a reorientation of their economic and social priorities.

In the event, the PCI found its campaign for the first direct election of the European Parliament overshadowed by the impact and preoccupations of the Italian general election which took place a week before the Italian electorate were asked to return to the polls for European Parliamentary elections. In the absence of any significant differences among the parties on European themes, interest turned on whether the PCI would fall any further behind the Christian Democrats compared with their performances in the general election. The PCI, in fact, with 29·6 per cent of the vote in the European elections was only very slightly down (on a lower poll) on its vote in the general election and took 24 of Italy's 81 seats. If anything, the Christian Democrats fared slightly worse, losing just over two per cent of their general election total but still taking six more seats than the PCI in the new European Parliament.

The PCF's handling of the question of direct elections has triggered some discussion concerning its internal procedures and its overall political image in France. Until April, 1977 the party fiercely opposed the direct election of the European Parliament on the fundamental grounds that the Parliament was claiming powers which could never be surrendered by national parliaments. Direct elections would be merely a further endorsement and legitimation of a thoroughly capitalist, even anti-French organisation. The PCF's sudden reversal of its position, made known in a French television interview with Marchais on April 17 (to the surprise of many rank and file) was more a

---

[10]See speech by Nilde Jotti, member of PCI delegation to European Parliament to Italian Chamber of Deputies, 11 February, 1977 published in *The Italian Communists* (foreign bulletin of the PCI), No. 1, January-March 1977.

reflection of the spin-off from the issue in French domestic politics, including the competition with the Socialist party in the Union of the Left, than a wholesale change of party convictions concerning the Parliament itself or the European Community.[11] Once it became clear from the attitudes of the other Member States and from the balance of political opinion in France (in spite of vehement Gaullist opposition) that direct elections would go ahead, there seemed little for the PCF to lose in ceasing to oppose the elections themselves; indeed, the party could probably not afford to miss the opportunity of matching itself with the Socialists in the electoral campaign. Being well aware of its apparent inconsistency, and sensitive to allegations concerning its political opportunism, the party, in the run-up to and during the campaign, vociferously condemned any increase in the powers of a directly-elected European Parliament and joined with the most determined of the Gaullist supporters of Jacques Chirac in warning against any further encroachment on French national sovereignty. In what was intended as a comparison unfavourable to the Socialist party, the PCF persistently claimed fidelity to the Union of the Left's Common Programme; thus, 'As intransigent defenders of national independence, the Communist deputies will do all in their power to preserve French freedom of action within the EEC. The French law (for direct elections) forbids, thanks to the action of the Communist deputies in particular, any increase in the powers of the European Assembly and any submission to the decisions of an external authority. The Communist deputies in the European Assembly will make sure that is scrupulously observed.[12]

The European elections in France, as in Italy, came to be seen much more as a test of relative party strengths in domestic terms than as a real test of attitudes towards the European Parliament and the European Community. Given the conflict between the PCF and the French Socialist party, following the post-electoral recriminations, most attention focussed on their performance relative to one another. The PCF managed to reproduce almost exactly its 20 per cent share of the votes won in the 1978 general election, taking 19 of the 81 French seats, while the Socialists, in alliance with the small Mouvement des Radicaux de Gauche lost some one per cent of their 1978 total and fell behind the PCF in some Departments which had proved more favourable to the Socialists in 1978.

The PCF's opposition to any extension of the European Parliament's role and authority finds no echo in the PCI or PCE. Indeed, the PCI regards an increase in the Parliament's powers, vis-à-vis the Council of Ministers in particular, as vital to the acceptability of the European Community as a whole and a necessary element in the reform of major policy areas. The gap between the two parties made their collaboration in a joint electoral campaign for the first round of elections somewhat problematical. It would appear to raise all

---

[11]See the article by Raymond Barrillon, 'Une double évolution avant de débats du Parlement', *Le Monde*, 19 April, 1977.

[12]Declaration of PCF, 7 April, 1978, author's translation.

sorts of difficulties for the future, should they find themselves in government and facing one another across the negotiating table in the Council of Ministers.

Some of the differences and contrasting expectations reflected in the parties' reactions to institutional questions not surprisingly overspill into their responses to the European Community's policy activities. These turn largely on the need to involve or defer to the Community in those policy areas which are regarded as crucial to the advance to socialism. There is substantial agreement at a declaratory level among all three parties on the need to redirect Community goals to correspond more closely with the interests of labour, and the need to undertake a much more drastic redistribution of resources to even out gross income and regional disparities. There is also universal agreement that the Community framework can best be justified (or, rather, for the PCF, reasonably tolerated) to the extent that it can exercise effective control over the activities of multinational companies. In more specific terms, however, the parties have generally left open the question of the precise division of labour between the European Community and the powers and instruments necessary for implementing socialist objectives at the national level. The PCF, in its criticisms of a wide range of existing Community policies, appears to be least prepared to consider alternatives which would not at the same time threaten to open up the fundamental relationship between the Member States and the Community. The PCI, on the other hand, has tended to focus more on pointing out the inadequacy and economic injustice of the integration process as it has so far developed. In so doing, it has indicated both its preferences for reform of some existing policies and suggested priorities for further policy initiatives where it envisages an essential and effective Community contribution. In the first category, the PCI, while not, of course, alone in advocating of reform has pressed, in both the national and the Community context, for substantial modifications to the Common Agricultural Policy (CAP) irrespective of further enlargement.[13] The party has condemned the distortions and expense of the CAP's pricing and intervention mechanisms, compounded by the inability of Italy's agricultural producers to supply their own market through the existence of monetary compensation amounts. In support of a national initiative to undertake a major reform of Italian agriculture, the PCI has proposed a combination of Community and national measures to be adopted in parallel through the CAP. These would include the introduction of national production quotas within the CAP to enable countries to meet a greater proportion of their own market needs and to take the responsibility for absorbing surpluses which may develop. At the Community level, the proposals include some use of direct income support from Community funds to assist farmers undertaking modernisation programmes, and more effective integration and a regionally sensitive emphasis in the application of agricultural policies with retraining schemes and industrial

---

[13]PCI Executive Committee Document, 'How the EEC's Agricultural Policy must be Revised', April 3, 1978, published in *The Italian Communists,* No. 2, July-August 1977.

policy initiatives. Examples where the PCI has pressed, in principle, for the development of Community policies, in the light of what the party sees as the inadequacy of national instruments, include monetary and energy policies, investment in advanced technology, and environmental policy. Given the assumptions and preferences of the PCF both in relation to the European Community and to national economic policy making, it would appear most unlikely that the PCI could look to a future joint set of Communist proposals to establish a Community presence in these policy areas.

In an interesting parallel with the issue of direct elections, the parties differing assessments of the relevance of the Community framework have been revealed in a striking way in their reactions to the prospect of Greek, Spanish and Portuguese membership of the European Community. Further enlargement triggers a number of policy and more general political consequences which have once again found the PCI and PCE on the opposite sides of the fence to the PCF. The PCE's endorsement of Spain's membership application, and the objectives of the post-Fascist regime in Spain *vis-à-vis* Western Europe, have posed a problem for calculations of party loyalties and estimates of political and economic advantage and vulnerability. The PCI, although recognising the existence of conflicts with Italian agricultural interests and greater competition for the meagre resources of the Community's Social and Regional Funds, has positively welcomed the inclusion of all three Mediterranean countries. It has preferred to see their challenge to the existing balance of economic interests as a lever for change rather than an excuse to delay their entry and lose the opportunity in the future of adding to the representation of 'progressive' forces at the Community level. The official PCF position has been to oppose vigorously the candidatures of Greece, Portugal and Spain, especially the latter. The party has undertaken an active, even populist anti-enlargement campaign within France, the more so as the French government's initial welcoming of enlargement has been seen to waver before the pressure of domestic economic interests.[14] The PCF's own negative response shows every sign of the need to defer to an important electoral constituency in weighing the merits of enlargement (as seen by the PCI) with the threats to the employment and income of a section of the party's support among southern French wine and agricultural producers. Indeed, the party's analyses of the reasons for, and implications of, enlargement suggest an almost exclusive concentration on the anticipated extension of multinational business activity into the enlarged market area, and the disruptive economic effects for French workers and peasants, with scarcely even a ritual acknowledgement of the political issues involved.

Given the above mixture of expectations, constructive criticisms and lingering suspicions, what can be said of the parties' conception of the role of the European Community in the achievement of national political and economic change and the fulfilment of their wider external objectives? One

[14]See Declaration of PCF on the enlargement of the European Community, 26 July 1977 and *L'Humanité,* 27 July, 1977.

characteristic of PCI rhetoric frequently applied to the analysis of the conditions for socialism in Italy is the argument that 'the problem of a new model of development of a democratic economic programme is no longer solely Italian, but it is, increasingly, West European.'[15] If translated into Community terms, this suggests the party's readiness, in the future, to envisage a close and necessary inter-connection between national and Community measures in the implementation of radical economic reform. In the meantime, and in the absence of a more democratic and sympathetic political framework, the PCI has been suspicious of the Community's potential for political interference in attempting to shape national choices, particularly in the economically weaker member states. Thus, the party strongly objected to the alleged infringement of Italian independence resulting from the conditions attached to the Community loan to Italy in March, 1976. Its misgivings were strengthened by the warnings from West Germany, France and Britain during the Puerto Rican economic summit that their willingness to give economic assistance to Italy would not remain unaffected in the event of PCI participation in government. The time lag between any future PCI involvement in government and the hoped-for political change throughout the rest of the Member States is likely to be such as to heighten the sensitivities of the party over any moves which would effectively limit the room for manoeuvre at the national level.

It is difficult to detect in the position of the PCF any signs that the party has thought in terms of an active contribution of the Community to the construction of socialism in France. All the political and economic indicators tend to point in the opposite direction. Unlike the PCI and PCE, the PCF has not looked to the Community as a supporting framework for political change in the sense of exploiting an opportunity at the regional level to mobilise a broad coalition of 'progressive forces'. Far from sharing the enthusiasm of the PCI for this reflection of its national political strategy, the PCF has been much more aware of the evident weakness of Communist parties, measured in regional terms by comparison with their relative strength at the national level. It has therefore, seen no particular advantage in terms of its national goals (and especially its preoccupation with preserving its own role and identity) in exploring the potential common ground amongst the political stands represented at the Community level.

Given the patchwork of attitudes and positions behind the three parties' common endorsement of the European Community their presence in government would present different problems and possibilities of adaptation, conciliation and/or confrontation for the Community as a whole and for individual Member States. Between the two extremes of repudiation on the one hand, and enthusiastic commitment to the existing Community 'package' on the other, there is room for varying degrees of support and criticism which could co-exist in the influence which the Communist parties might bring to bear. Towards the positive end of the scale, the overall importance attached to

---

[15]Sergio Segre (International Affairs section of PCI) quoted in D. Sassoon, *op. cit.*, p. 30.

entry into the European Community in Spanish domestic politics and foreign policy, in the light of the post-Franco political debate, is likely to sustain the PCE's identification with the principle, if not every detail, of Spanish membership. In Italy and France, the demands of the historic compromise strategy and Left coalition politics, both involving compromises with traditionally pro-integration parties, will provide one set of pressures justifying toleration of the European Community. Towards the negative end of the scale, the parties' concern to keep open domestic economic options in anticipation of future opportunities for radical change, would make them unsympathetic, if not hostile, to attempts to step up the pace of economic integration.

A combination of positive and negative components in the attitudes and policies of governments is not, of course, unfamilar in the Community framework. Even in the absence of PCI, PCF or PCE participation in government it could not be said that the European Community enjoys a complete and unshakeable consensus in relation to its existing activities and future goals. The experience of absorbing the critical approach of the British Labour government since 1974 provides one example of the Community's response to attempted change at the national level. The Labour Government's renegotiation of the terms of Britain's membership, and its strategy of attrition in a number of policy areas have not been presented as a systematic ideological challenge to the Community. Nevertheless, they have been interpreted as persistent questioning of basic Community principles. A characteristic of the Community's response to Britain's criticisms, caution and obstructiveness has been the handling of the contentious issues in a piecemeal fashion. This has been influenced partly by a concern to contain differences within the overall Community framework and to maintain British involvement in this, and partly by the assessment that Britain's approach does not represent the external arm of a programme designed to initiate profound internal political, economic and social change.

Indeed, the PCI's attitude to the Community's institutional development demonstrates some confidence in the role of the Commission which the latter might hope to build on in confirming the PCI in its conversion to the Community and to the further growth of Community institutional authority. The overall stance of the PCF is likely to be more explicitly critical, though the manner and extent of its resistance to Community 'interference' is likely to be shaped by perception of domestic priorities and the pace of its reform programme, rather than any pressure to provoke an immediate confrontation.

The capacity of the European Community to 'absorb' the impact of Communist participation in government depends not only on the postures adopted by the parties themselves, but also on the perceptions and the congruence in the attitudes of individual Member States. In this sense, the British example may not be an appropriate one. Opinion within the Community was reasonably united (if not agreed on every issue) in attempting to accommodate the demands made by the British Labour Government in 1974

73

and 1975. Projections of future responses to Communist party positions need to take into account the possibility of specific and differing national or party political instincts. Whether these reactions would amount to a divisive or a unifying force within the Community framework would clearly depend on the political complexions of the governments of the time. So far the West German and British Governments, not least because of their current or recent social democratic complexion, have appeared the most sceptical of the strategies of the PCI, PCF and PCE and their potential contribution to government. How far their suspicions of Communist party motives and influence would carry over into their stances on Community questions is a moot point. Chancellor Schmidt has already indicated West German reluctance to endorse an Italian Government, with PCI representation, taking advantage of support available within the Community framework. On the other hand, it may not be entirely inconceivable that a future British Government, of whatever political complexion, might find itself torn between its political inhibitions and the prospect of potential allies in some aspects of Community policies and practices.

VI Conclusions

It is a striking thought that few discussions and analyses of Eurocommunism devote much time or space to foreign policy issues. They are usually dismissed with a passing reference to the limited changes which the parties have made in relation to the Atlantic Alliance and the European Community, with the rider that on all other matters the parties have remained faithful to the Soviet Union. Compared with alterations in their domestic strategies, and their identification with democratic principles, modifications to a restricted area of foreign policy either appear less portentous, or else point immediately to the USSR as the lynch-pin of the parties' identity and cohesion. This study has not sought directly to explore in detail the precise significance of the USSR to the current positions or future roles of the PCI, PCF and PCE. Rather, it has attempted to examine the parties' exploitation of a limited part of the foreign policy arena as one means by which they could increase their influence and ultimately their representation in government.

If assertions of independence from the USSR have been taken as one fundamental aspect of Eurocommunism, some degree of convergence in the attitudes and policies of the West European Communist parties has frequently been seen as another major feature. In foreign policy, at least in those areas where the parties' positions have undergone some change, convergence amongst all three parties has been less noticeable than the surfacing of competing views. These are traceable to differences in conceptions of the issues themselves (as on aspects of the European Community) to party interpretations of national preoccupations and priorities (defence) and estimates of domestic coalition needs. Total convergence in attitudes and strategies does not, of course, exist in the domestic sphere. Here a number of observers have noted the permutations of party links in relation to different areas.[1] In foreign policy more often than not, the PCI and PCE share a similar perspective with which the PCF appears to have little in common.

The evaluation of foreign policy issues in the context of the political progress and adaptation of the three Communist parties can be approached in

---

[1]See, for example, analysis of Eurocommunism themes in A. Kriegel, *Un Autre Communisme?*, Hachette, Paris, 1977.

two ways. The first involves the relevance and integration of foreign policy changes *vis-à-vis* the parties' overall political stances and, including not least, their relevance for the continuing link with the USSR. The second poses questions concerning the likelihood and the extent of foreign policy change in the event of Communist party participation in government. These touch on the coherence and direction of the foreign policies which emerge from both the changes and the continuity in party attitudes.

The relevance of foreign policy for understanding the changes in the PCI, PCF and PCE varies according to one's emphasis and perspective. We have already noted that foreign policy issues have had both contextual and pro-grammatic significance for the parties. While detente has provided the essential conditions which enable the parties to consider alternative domestic strategies, foreign policy issues in themselves have not, on the whole, been central to their campaigns. They have held limited electoral appeal, even though in the case of the PCI, they have been more important in the formulating of long term plans for collaboration with other political parties. From the point of view of the Communist parties, inasmuch as they perceive that independence of the USSR is an important factor in increasing their support, the foreign policy terrain has proved more difficult and less productive than other areas. Although all three parties have made use of some foreign policy issues to enhance their overall national legitimacy and acceptability, there have been scarcely any examples where flexibility in internal party structures and discipline have surfaced in foreign policy debate. On the other hand, from an external viewpoint, the parties' moves to tone down their previous outright rejection of the assumptions behind the alliance and institutional ties and commitments of Western European states are not without significance or interest. The parties have regarded these moves (in part) as necessary signals and evidence of their concern to try to avoid antagonism and suspicion of a kind which might make their future regimes vulnerable to external intervention.

The integration of changes in foreign policy into the rest of the parties' political programmes is partly a question of consistency, and partly a reflection of the relationship which each party envisages in broad terms between foreign policy and domestic change. A striking feature here is the difference in approach and assumptions between the PCI and the PCF. If the party's rhetoric is taken as a guide, the PCI's advocacy of Western Europe's assertion of regional autonomy and distinctiveness at the international level, and its justification for extending its national political strategy to the regional level are designed to complement and reinforce one another. Changes in foreign policy at both the national and regional levels are not merely supportive but essential ingredients in the completion and safeguarding of the PCI's domestic objectives. By contrast, the PCF appears much less at ease within the regional dimension and unconvinced that the transition to socialism in France would need to be fitted into a wider framework. The party's emphasis on national autonomy in foreign policy and its lack of enthusiasm for regional initiatives indicate a much more self-contained assessment of the link between foreign policy and domestic political change.

Almost irrespective of the perspective or focus in studies of the evolution of the PCI, PCF and PCE, it is the relationship with the USSR which frequently emerges in the last analysis as both the most important and the most tantalising of the factors determining the significance of party changes. The relationship in foreign policy touches on one of the most fundamental aspects of West European Communist parties' attitude towards the Soviet Union: their readiness to support Soviet foreign policy objectives in Western Europe and more generally on international issues. The parties' shifts of position have disturbed, though still far from completely undermined, this basic response. Again, the distinction holds up between the postures of the PCI and PCE on the one hand, and the PCF on the other in terms of the challenge they present to Soviet aims. If reservations noted earlier are allowed for, the more positive endorsement of the European Community by the PCI and PCE, and their inclination to assert the virtues of Western Europe's regional autonomy against the danger of American and Soviet hegemony can scarcely have been welcome to the Soviet Union. By comparison, the PCF's modifications to its views on the Atlantic Alliance and European Community, preoccupied as it has been to defend national autonomy, have provoked less concern on the part of the USSR. Alternatively, in the case of the retention of the 'force de frappe', the PCF's position is probably regarded as sufficiently qualified not to pose a significant threat.[2] One is also tempted to wonder whether uncertainty over the level of the PCI's involvement in NATO as well as the highly circumscribed adherence of the PCF to the Alliance indicate that any Soviet reaction might be more displeasure at symbolic 'defections' than fear of the practical consequences.

The convergence of views between the parties and the USSR on a range of foreign policy questions which impinge both on revolutionary issues and Soviet influence in various parts of the world indicate the persistence of some common perspectives and (at least declared) objectives. The extent to which these point to the existence of identifiable boundaries to the parties' evolution in foreign policy is not yet clear. So far domestic strategies appear to have provided a major criteria for judging the extent of independence asserted in relation to Soviet foreign policy. Thus, on those issues which belong, in Pierre Hassner's phrase, to the more 'romantic and moral' aspects of the Communist parties' foreign policies, it is arguable that the parties have judged their domestic importance to be low, whilst their 'visibility' in terms of their relations with the USSR is relatively high.[3] How far these calculations would survive the entry of the Communist parties into government could only be

<hr />

[2]On the acceptability of PCF views on foreign policy see H. Adomeit, 'Moscow, Europe and Eurocommunism', paper presented to Annual Meeting of Canadian Political Science Association, London, Ontario, 28 May, 1978.

[3]P. Hassner, 'L'Avenir des Alliances en Europe', paper delivered to IPSA Congress, Edinburgh, August 1976.

answered in the light of information on the future pressures and sensitivities on both sides concerning the maintenance of harmonious relations. The possibilities of foreign policy dissent have begun to be explored. Outside of government the parties' abilities to strike a balance between loyalties and conflicting political assessments, and to defer the practical consequences of their differences with the USSR, have so far contained this dissent within a relatively narrow area. Inside government, the choices facing the parties may be more demanding and explicit, and less susceptible, therefore, to the cautious pace of change adopted hitherto.

Speculation over the impact on foreign policy in Western Europe of Communist participation in government is subject to a number of uncertainties in addition to the Soviet factor already referred to. Domestic political variables, such as estimates of the weight of the PCF in a future French Communist-Socialist coalition, the potential clash between a Left government and a more conservative Presidency and the compromises emerging from possible variants of coalition politics involving the PCI (and, conceivably, the PCE in the future) would need to be fitted into assessments of possible changes. Speculation by potentially-affected governments which anticipate unwelcome change has characterised the political debate surrounding the increasing influence of the Communist parties. In this debate, the lead has undoubtedly, and in foreign policy terms not surprisingly, been taken by the United States. Although the Carter Administration has modified the uncompromising tactics adopted by Henry Kissinger and the Ford Administration, the official American response to the prospect of PCI or PCF participation in government has demonstrated a wide-ranging preoccupation with the assumed harmful domestic and foreign policy consequences. These have been seen principally as presenting a threat to internal democratic institutions, posing serious difficulties for the military and political cohesion of the Atlantic Alliance and undermining domestic support in the United States for continued American commitment to the Alliance in its present form.

The assumptions underpinning the American reaction to potential Communist influence over foreign policy suggest that, irrespective of the extent of the parties' independence from the USSR, their domestic and foreign policy objectives would lead to a radical change of emphasis in foreign policy and greater fragmentation of interests in Western Europe. Assessments of this kind depend, in part, on interpretations of the overall direction and priorities in the foreign policies of the PCI, PCF and PCE in the light of the changes they have introduced, and the survival of attitudes and reflexes which sit rather uncomfortably next to their newly modified positions. The policies of the three parties reveal the co-existence of four potential 'points of reference' which are likely to shape their approach in the future. These are firstly, an underlying reserve of support for the broad objectives of Soviet foreign policy, secondly the assertion of specific national objectives, thirdly a guarded tolerance of the Atlantic link and, fourthly, an awareness though not, as yet, an unconditional endorsement, of the regional dimension in Western Europe. There is clearly plenty of scope for conflict amongst these four points which could determine the impact that the Communist parties would have in particular areas of foreign policy.

On the whole, expectations of the short term policy repercussions of Communist participation in government have largely reflected the assumption that the first two 'reference points'—the Soviet focus and the assertion of national goals—will prevail in the attitudes of the parties. Depending on the institutional context and the issue, the major preoccupations have centred on the reliability, obstructiveness or indifference of the parties and the challenge which they are thus seen to present to an existing consensus or balance of interests. In the case of NATO, these preoccupations have been widely voiced in terms of the ability to maintain the confidentiality of sensitive military and political information in the event of PCI participation in government; and more broadly, if governments with PCI and PCF representation were to remain within the Atlantic Alliance, the likelihood of 'psychological malaise' besetting other participants and NATO commanders. In the case of the European Community, the concern has been the loss of momentum resulting from persistent obstructiveness or simply indifference, and the pressures which might be triggered off in other Member States by a rapid resort to import controls and export aids as part of measures by the Communist parties to reorganise their economies.

On the other hand, in the light of some of the points made in previous chapters, it is arguable that countervailing factors may well exist which would indicate that such expectations might be unduly alarmist. In the NATO context, as a number of observers have pointed out, it is clear that the problem of information leakage is not exclusive to Communist parties.[4] Perhaps more significantly, the PCI has demonstrated in a number of ways its awareness of its vulnerability to charges of prejudicing 'national interests'. The political risks involved in the PCI fulfilling the expectations of its most suspicious critics would be very great. Within the European Community, it is apparent that the responses of the three Communist parties would not all point in the same direction. The PCI and PCE appear to find some positive features in the Community framework which they might be expected actively to exploit. The PCF would be the least likely to adopt a co-operative attitude, although the extent of its potentially negative influence and the expected clash over the demands of domestic economic reform would depend very much on the overall party and political balance within a Communist-Socialist coalition.

Even without direct Communist participation in government, the awareness of both the Italian and French Governments of the political challenge from the Left and the Left's ability to exploit doubts and misgivings associated with the defence of national interests or resistance to American penetration, has

---

[4]See Ciro Zoppa, 'The Military Policies of the Italian Communist Party', *Survival*, Vol. XX, March/April 1978. For contrary arguments see J. Dougherty and D. Pfaltzgraff, *Eurocommunism and the Atlantic Alliance*, Institute for Foreign Policy Analysis, Cambridge, Massachusetts, 1977.

increased their sensitivity in those multilateral arenas where governments are subject to public scrutiny. In France, the Giscard d'Estaing Presidency has already appeared concerned that the PCF's criticism of its Atlanticist leanings in foreign and defence policy could have damaging consequences for its desired image of vigorously defending French independence and preserving French initiative. The Christian Democratic Government in Italy has seemed even more vulnerable to PCI criticism of its lack of assertiveness in foreign policy. On defence expenditure and efficiency, in developing Italy's specific interests in the Mediterranean area within the framework of the Atlantic Alliance, and especially in its arguments in favour of greater civilian accountability of the armed forces, the PCI's vigorous campaigning has pointedly revealed the complacency and inertia which it associates with a too-long period of unchallenged Christian Democratic control of foreign policy.

The existence of some countervailing factors which suggest that the Communist parties would not necessarily fulfil the totally disruptive role frequently expected of them does not, of course, imply willing accommodation on their part with existing foreign policy assumptions or priorities. This study has tried to indicate the major areas where differences persist and where attempts would be made by Communist-influenced governments to reshape the orientation of existing foreign policies and, in particular, to try to reduce the importance which multilateral arenas have come to hold in the foreign policy of Western European states.

On one level the foreign policy strategies associated with Eurocommunism can be presented merely as devices designed either to bolster domestic images or, in a Machiavellian sense, eventually to undermine the 'solidarity' of Western European interests in preparation for a more fundamental confrontation. On another level, however, and taking them for this purpose somewhat at their face value, they could also be seen as attempts to explore the possibilities for change within a set of (international) constraints which appear (like domestic parliamentary institutions and preferences for democratic liberties) too costly to break with completely.

In fact, for the PCI, PCF and PCE, the 'constraints' are of two kinds and their room for safe manoeuvre in relation to both is still uncertain. One set consists of an awareness of the need to maintain a so-called 'equilibrium' in international politics and the demands made by a changing international network of economic interests. The other comes from the opposite direction in the shape of the influence of the USSR—generally seen to date as being more powerful. The ways in which these constraints are presented and perceived by the parties in the future, particularly in the application of pressure either by the United States and other West European governments, or by the USSR itself, will be crucial. They would largely determine the ability of the Communist parties to match their attempts to project the possibility of a peaceful transition to socialism at the national level with the prospect of controlling the direction of change at the international level. This would require a Communist-influenced government to have the confidence and ability to manage those aspects of its foreign policy which could be crucial to its domestic and international credibility and survival. The handling of the Soviet relationship, in both its ideological and external diplomatic aspects will be a vital, but still relatively unpredictable factor. So, too, would be the capacity of a Communist government to control the reactions and doubts emanating from the key economic and strategic forums of the European Community and the Atlantic Alliance. Together, these elements would add up to an ability on the part of the Communist parties to hold a major part of their international environment stable while they achieved the desired degree of domestic change. Bearing in mind that the parties have also to cast an eye to their status as proponents of revolutionary situations in parts of the world where the conditions are considered ripe, such a balance between even declared revolutionary zeal and a responsible and cautious image in European relations will be immensely difficult to sustain.

Reports already published

The POLICY STUDIES INSTITUTE (PSI) is a British independent policy research organisation concerned with issues relevant to economic and social policies and the working of political institutions.

PSI was formed in April 1978 through the merger of Political and Economic Planning (PEP), founded in 1931, and the Centre for Studies in Social Policy (CSSP), founded in 1972. It continues the tradition of both organisations to establish the facts by impartial empirical research and to relate the findings to practical policy making. The scope of the Institute's work has been extended by the recent establishment of a European Centre for Political Studies. PSI's work is financed by grants for specific studies made by trusts, foundations and public bodies, with substantial support from donations by industry and commerce, and by annual subscriptions.

The results of the studies are disseminated widely by means of frequent publications, articles and seminars.

1-2 Castle Lane, London SW1E 6DR
Telephone: 01-828 7055

How to obtain PSI publications

PSI publications may be obtained from booksellers or direct from PSI. Postage and packing will be additional to the cost of the publication if it is sent by post.

A full list of recent publications and subscription details will be sent on request to PSI at 1-2 Castle Lane, London SW1E 6DR.